I0438966

NISTIR 7519

Style Guide for Voting System Documentation

Dana E. Chisnell
UsabilityWorks

Susan C. Becker
Codewords

Sharon J. Laskowski
Information Access Division
Information Technology Laboratory

Svetlana Z. Lowry
Information Access Division
Information Technology Laboratory

August, 2008

Contents

Style Guide for Voting System Documentation[1]

Background

This style guide is a product of the voting system standards and test methods research at the National Institute of Standards and Technology (NIST). NIST provides technical assistance to the Election Assistance Commission (EAC) and the Technical Guidelines Development Committee, an advisory group to the EAC as established by the Help America Vote Act of 2002.

The most recent version of the technical standard, the Voluntary Voting System Guidelines (VVSG) of August, 2007[2], contains requirements for the usability of documentation used by poll workers and election support staff.   Our approach to testing these requirements has two components:

1. Style guide incorporating best practices for voting system documentation

2. Test protocol for voting system test laboratories to use to measure the usability of instructions supplied by voting system manufacturers for election workers

This document is the style guide, which sets out guidelines for voting system manufacturers to use to implement best practices in their documentation for poll workers and election support staff. Ideally, these guidelines could eventually be incorporated in the VVSG, in a section equivalent to the direction already included for user interfaces of voting systems (Part 1: 3.2.4-C "Plain Language"). At the very least, they form a basis for voting system test laboratories to evaluate documentation.

---

[1] This document and associated files have been prepared by the National Institute of Standards and Technology (NIST) and represent draft test materials for the Election Assistance Commission's next iteration of the VVSG. It is a preliminary draft and does not represent a consensus view or recommendation from NIST, nor does it represent any policy positions of NIST.

Certain commercial entities, equipment, or material may be identified in the document in order to describe an experimental procedure or concept adequately. Such identification is not intended to imply recommendation or endorsement by the National Institute of Standards and Technology, nor is it intended to imply that these entities, materials, or equipment are necessarily the best available for the purpose.

[2] http://vote.nist.gov/vvsg-report.htm

The second component, a test protocol for voting system test laboratories for testing instructions with typical election workers to detect flaws in the instructions is currently under development at NIST.

To develop the guidelines, we reviewed:

- Research related to technical communication and information design. This review resulted in *Review of relevant literature: technical communication and information design* (Chisnell and Becker 2007a).

- Existing guidelines from government agencies and other groups. This review resulted in *Current guidelines: technical communication and information design* (Chisnell and Becker 2007b).

- Documentation developed by voting system manufacturers that is directed to poll workers. We based our review on what we learned from our reviews of the research and guidelines in current use. This review resulted in *Gaps between voting system documentation and best practice in technical communication and information design* (Chisnell and Becker 2008a).

- The 2007 VVSG requirements for documentation for poll workers and for plain language in system instructions. This review resulted in *Applying best practice in technical communication and information design to documentation for poll workers* (Chisnell and Becker 2008b).

We also gathered information from voting system manufacturers about the people who write the voting system documentation. This helped us better understand the writers' tasks and constraints.

What is in this document

This document discusses guidelines for writing voting system documentation. It focuses on documentation for setting up voting systems, conducting polling, and shutting down and auditing voting systems.

Because poll workers usually perform these tasks, the guidelines and examples focus on writing documentation for poll workers. However, the guidelines apply to writing voting system documentation for all users.

These guidelines would add specificity to the VVSG in Part 2: Chapter 4: "Voting Equipment User Documentation (manufacturer)," as well as expand on points in Part 2: 3.1.1.1-C "TDP contents" and Part 1: 3.2.8

"Usability for poll workers," including Part 1: 3.2.8.1-C "Documentation usability."

How to use this document

Each guideline includes direction for voting system manufacturers to implement the guideline and to evaluate if it has been met. The discussion includes examples of typical mistakes in voting system documentation and suggestions of ways to revise.

We chose these best practice guidelines because:

- These guidelines can help writers solve many high-level problems that in turn eliminate typical, smaller problems.

- These guidelines are widely and consistently agreed upon and supported, based on the research we reviewed for this project.

- Testing methods are available to evaluate objectively whether these guidelines have been implemented effectively.

- Based on our experience as technical communicators and information designers, we believe these guidelines provide reasonable guidance that can fit into standard writing and review cycles.

Note: The examples used in this report are adapted for illustrative purposes and do not represent original documentation from voting system manufacturers.

Guidelines

Writing the documentation for specific users

- Understand your users
- Understand your users' tasks
- Address one group of users at a time

Organizing to meet your users' needs

- Focus on your users' tasks
- Organize the documentation logically and clearly
- Use informative headings

Using simple words your users understand

- Use familiar, common words

- Use consistent terminology
- Use gender neutral language

Writing directly to your users

- Use the imperative in instructions
- Use "you" when writing to your users
- Use the active voice

Keeping instructions short and simple

- Make each instruction a separate step
- Use numbers for steps
- Use bullets for lists
- Put steps in the order in which they must be completed
- Put information in a step in the order needed
- Put warnings before—not after—consequences
- Make each step as short as possible

Using graphics effectively

- Use graphics to illustrate tasks
- Make the relationship between graphics and text clear
- Keep graphics simple—show only what is necessary
- Identify items and actions on graphics

Designing the documentation for easy scanning and reading

- Use informative headers and footers
- Design pages for easy scanning and reading

Testing the documentation

Writing the documentation for specific users

The documentation set for a voting system can cover information for several different groups of users including election administrators, information technology workers, local elections officials, election judges, various clerks, and general poll workers.

The tasks and motivations of each group of users are different. For example, election administrators may review documentation to make decisions about purchasing systems, while poll workers refer to documents only if necessary to complete their tasks on Election Day.

When you write documentation for specific groups of users, each group can then understand and use their documentation more easily because it is shorter, simpler, and more appropriate. It contains only as much information as they need, when they need it, in language they can understand.

For example, the poll worker's guide addresses poll workers–the people who run polling places on Election Day, including clerks and election judges. It covers only their tasks on that day.

To write the documentation for specific users:

- Understand your users
- Understand your users' tasks
- Address one group of users at a time

Understand your users

Know your users, for example, election support staff, such as poll workers, clerks, and election judges.

What? To understand your users, you need specific information:

- Demographics: age, education, work and life experience

- Motivation and compensation

- Experience working on elections

- Previous knowledge of voting systems

- Previous knowledge of elections and election terminology

- Physical ability, if their tasks involve physical work

How?

- Visit polling places on Election Day:

  - Be a poll worker.

  - Vote at your polling place.

  - Observe a polling place.

- Read research reports and news articles about poll workers.

- Create personas of your users (composite representations of typical users). Use them as you develop and evaluate the documentation. (See the resources on page 67.)

- Test the documentation to make sure it speaks to your users. (See page 62.)

- Document your understanding of your users with an audience analysis or profile in the document project plan (but not the documentation itself).

Good example. This step from a poll worker's guide tells poll workers what to do in simple terms.

5. On the Access Code slip, check the voter's precinct I.D.

Revising. This note from a poll worker's guide includes terminology and information that most poll workers do not understand. No matter how the voting equipment is set up, the poll workers only need to know when to print the zero report.

Before

Note: The election definition determines if the zero report reflects an individual terminal or all open terminals.

After

Note: When you open the last terminal, print the zero report.

Why? When you know your audience, you can address them more effectively in these ways:

- Use language and terminology they understand.
- Include information they need and leave out what they already know.
- Break complex tasks into simpler steps suitable for the context.

Evaluation checklist

This guideline (understand your users) does not have any specific items on the evaluation checklist. But it affects how successfully the documentation meets all the other items.

Understand your users' tasks

Know your users' tasks; for example, if your users are the poll workers, know their main tasks for Election Day and all the steps involved in completing those tasks successfully.

What? The users' tasks are the actions they need to take to do their job or accomplish their goals. For example, the VVSG (Voluntary Voting System Guidelines), in Part 1:3.2.8.1 "Operation," defines the poll workers' tasks as:

- Setting up and opening the polls, including setting up the equipment, but not defining the ballots

- Running the polls during voting hours, including:

  - Checking voter identification and authorization

  - Preparing the system for the next voter

  - Assisting voters who need help

  - Performing routine operations like installing a new roll of paper

- Closing and shutting down the polls so that no more votes are cast

How?

- Visit polling places on Election Day:

  - Be a poll worker.

  - Vote at your polling place.

  - Observe a polling place.

- Interview your users, for example, poll workers and election officials.

- Think through your users' tasks using their personas. For example, walk though Election Day using your poll worker personas to develop a list of all the required tasks. (See the resources on page 67.)

- Talk with the designers and developers of the polling equipment to learn how it works.

- Document your understanding of your users' tasks with a task analysis, based on your research, in the document project plan.

Good example. See the example for "Understand your users" on page 9.

Revising. In this poll worker's guide, the first step of the day tells the poll workers to contact the manufacturer. The task of inspecting and replacing the cord is not the poll workers' job. Other staff must solve this problem.

Before

Opening the Polls

1. Inspect the power cord for damage.

   If the cord is damaged, discard it and contact the manufacturer for a new cord.

After

Opening the Polls

1. Inspect the power cord for damage.

   If the cord is damaged, contact Election Central.

Why? When you understand your users' tasks, you can develop the documentation to cover the specific information they need to do their jobs. See "Focus on your users' tasks" on page 16.

Evaluation checklist

This guideline (understand your users' tasks) does not have any specific items on the evaluation checklist. But it affects how successfully the documentation meets all the other items.

Address one group of users at a time

Write to one group of users at a time. Include only the information that group needs to complete their tasks.

What? Provide information and instructions for one group of users at a time, rather than including information for different groups in the same paragraph, set of instructions, or chapter. For example, in the poll worker's guide, include only the information that poll workers need to complete their tasks on Election Day.

How?

- Address one specific group of users in a document or major section of the documentation.

- In a specific document or major section, include only the information that the users you are addressing need to complete their tasks.

- Make the poll worker's guide a separate document rather than including it as a chapter in a multipurpose guide.

- In a poll worker's guide, include only the information that poll workers need to complete their tasks.

- As much as possible, put information for each group of users in separate documents specifically for those users; for example, put information for the IT staff in an operator's guide.

See also

- Understand your users' tasks (page 11)
- Focus on your users' tasks (page 16)
- Use the imperative in instructions (page 29)
- Use "you" when writing to your users (page 30)

Good example. This statement from an introduction to a setup guide defines the audience (poll workers), speaks directly to them using "you," and describes the task from their point of view.

About this guide	This guide provides you with the instructions for setting up voting equipment in a polling place.
Audience	Election Judges (Poll Workers)

Revising. This operations manual includes one chapter for poll workers; the rest is for information technology (IT) staff.

Before

Chapter 5: Pre-Election Day Preparation
Chapter 6: Poll Worker Election Day Procedures
Chapter 7: Post-Election Tasks

After

Chapter 5: Pre-Election Day Preparation
Chapter 6: Post-Election Tasks

Poll Worker Election Day Procedures (a stand-alone document)

Why? Addressing more than one audience in a single document adds complexity for each audience. Multipurpose documents or documents that attempt to serve multiple audiences are difficult for almost anyone to use to find what they need to accomplish their goals.

Evaluation checklist

☐ Does the documentation address one group of users at a time?

☐ Does each document or major section include only the information needed by the group of users it addresses?

☐ Is the poll worker's guide a separate document rather than a chapter in a multipurpose guide?

☐ Does the poll worker's guide include only the information that poll workers need?

Tip! In a poll worker's guide, include tasks that are completed on Election Day, not before or after. (These tasks probably belong to someone other than a poll worker.)

Organizing to meet your users' needs

When information is presented logically from the users' point of view, they can find the information they need, fit it into what they already know, and use it to complete their tasks.

Some tasks can be completed and then forgotten. For example, poll workers can follow the instructions to print the opening reports, and then forget about that task. If they need the information again, they can find it more easily in documentation that is clearly organized.

Other tasks need to be repeated many times. For example, poll workers may need to process provisional ballots throughout Election Day. Users can remember the information more easily if it is organized with related ideas and tasks together. Or if they forget the information, they can find it again more easily in documentation that is organized based on their tasks.

To organize the documentation to meet your users' needs:

- Focus on your users' tasks
- Organize the documentation logically and clearly
- Use informative headings

Focus on your users' tasks

Focus on what your users need to do to complete a task rather than on what the system is doing (or can do).

What? The users' tasks are the actions they need to take to complete their job or accomplish their goals. For example, the poll workers' tasks on Election Day in general are:

- Setting up and opening the polls

- Running the polls

- Closing and shutting down the polls

How?

- Explain how to complete the tasks instead of describing the voting system.

- Describe only the relevant parts of voting system when the users need to understand them to complete a task, rather than in overviews.

See also

- Understand your users' tasks (page 11)

- Use the imperative in instructions (page 29)

Good example. These instructions from a poll worker's guide describe what the poll workers need to do—turn on and secure a voting machine.

1. Open the Polls Open/Closed switch cover.

2. Remove the red seal from inside and set it aside.

3. Turn the Polls Open/Closed switch to the Open position.

4. Close the Polls Open/Closed switch cover.

5. Secure the Polls Open/Closed switch cover with the red seal.

Revising. This step from a poll worker's guide describes the equipment (the color-coded plugs) rather than what poll workers need to do to set up the equipment.

Before

1. Note that there are two plugs. These two plugs are color-coded so that you plug them correctly into the power supply. The plugs with the red and yellow dots are plugged into the power supply so that the dots on the power supply match the dots on the plugs.

After

1. Insert the plug with the red dot into the power supply outlet with the red dot.

2. Insert the plug with the yellow dot into the power supply outlet with the yellow dot.

Why? Most readers scan until they find an action and then take the first reasonable action they see. When the system documentation describes the voting equipment rather than the tasks, the users have to figure out what to do from the description, rather than simply follow directions. They may need more time and make more errors.

Evaluation checklist

☐ Does the documentation explain how to complete the tasks rather than describe the voting equipment?

☐ Is voting equipment explained with the tasks, rather than in overviews?

Organize the documentation logically and clearly

Put the information in the order that your users need it.

How?

- Base the organization of the documentation on your analysis of the users' tasks. (See "Understand your users' tasks" page 11.)

- If the users complete the tasks in a particular order, organize the documentation based on that order.

- When chronological order is not important, organize by the importance or frequency of the tasks. Put the most important and most frequent tasks first.

- Organize the poll worker's guide chronologically, following the poll workers' tasks through Election Day.

Good example. In this poll worker's guide, the information is in the order that the poll workers need to complete the tasks.

> Setting Up
>
> > Positioning the Voting Units
> >
> > Setting Up the Voting Units
> >
> > Turning On the Power

Revising. In this poll worker's guide, the first heading covers 2 tasks (start up and shut down) that the poll workers complete 12 or more hours apart. It is based on the equipment: the unit can be started and shut down with the same switch.

> **Before**
>
> Start Up/Shut Down Procedure
>
> Setting Up the Unit for Voters
>
> Assisting the Voters
>
> **After**
>
> Starting the Unit
>
> Setting Up the Unit for Voters
>
> Assisting the Voters
>
> Shutting Down the Unit

Why? Users can find information quicker in a logically organized document. Chronological order is especially easy for users to understand. It is also appropriate for describing the activities and events of Election Day, which follow a set, time-based pattern of opening the polls, assisting voters, and closing the polls.

Evaluation checklist

☐ Is the documentation organized logically based on the user's tasks?

☐ If the users must complete the tasks in a particular order, is the document organized chronologically based on that order?

☐ When chronological order is not important, is the document organized by the importance or frequency of the tasks?

☐ Is the poll worker's guide in particular organized chronologically based on the poll workers' tasks?

Use informative headings

Use headings that help your users scan the documentation to find the information they need.

What? Informative headings describe each section of text or set of instructions and help users find the information they need.

How?

- Describe the users' tasks rather than the equipment.

- Use an effective form for headings:

  - Verbs and verb phrases: Determining if a voter is eligible.

  - Questions: How do I determine if a voter is eligible?

  - Sentences: Determine if the voter is eligible.

- Avoid nouns and noun phrases: Determination of voter eligibility.

- Make headings in a section grammatically parallel.

Good example. These headings from a poll worker's guide are verb phrases that describe the poll workers' tasks.

> Ending the Election
> > Counting Outstanding Ballots
> > Locking the Ballot Counter
> > Printing the Election Results Report
> > Turning off the Ballot Counter
> > Sending Election Results to Election Central

Revising. The first subheading is a noun phrase, which is less effective. Also, the headings are not parallel; the top level heading and the last subheading are verbs phrases (specifically gerunds). But the others are not. In the revision, the headings are all the same type of verb phrase.

Before

> Setting up the Voting Station
> > Assign Station Identification
> > Printer Set-Up
> > Testing the Voting Units

After

> Setting up the Voting Station
> > Assigning the Station Identification
> > Setting up the Printer
> > Testing the Voting Units

More revising. Here the headings from a poll worker's guide describe the voting equipment rather than the poll workers' tasks and use computer terminology (coding) rather than language the poll workers use.

Before

Loading a Ballot
    Poll Worker Ballot and Precinct Selection Screens
    Coding a ballot

After

Loading a Ballot
    Selecting a Precinct
    Selecting a Ballot
    Marking a Ballot to Review for Voter Eligibility

Why? Informative headings aid scanning by describing what each section discusses and by breaking large blocks of text into smaller chunks that cover a single topic.

Evaluation checklist

☐ Do the headings describe users' tasks rather than equipment?

☐ Are the headings in an effective form: verbs, questions, or sentences?

☐ Are the headings in a section grammatically parallel?

Tip! For the poll worker's guide, create a table of contents from the headings. They should read like a set of high level instructions that follow the poll workers' day.

Using simple words your users understand

The normal reading process involves both recognizing letters in a word and applying contextual information to recognize the word. Short words and familiar words are easier to recognize.

For example, if a poll worker's guide uses short, familiar words, poll workers can quickly read what they need and get back to their job of running the polls on Election Day.

To use simple words that your users understand:

- Use familiar, common words
- Use consistent terminology
- Use gender neutral language

Use familiar, common words

Use the words your users use. Particularly for poll worker documentation, avoid technical or specialized terminology that poll workers don't understand.

What? Words that are familiar and common for the general population are appropriate for poll worker documentation. For other system documentation, specific terminology that is familiar and common for those users is appropriate.

How?

- Use short, simple words.

- Select the plain, rather than the formal word.

- Describe voting equipment rather than using the manufacturer's name for it.

- Avoid unfamiliar election terminology.

- In poll worker documentation, avoid computer and software terminology.

- Explain unfamiliar terms when they appear, not only in a list of terms.

- Avoid acronyms and abbreviations; define them when you use them.

Good (and bad) examples

Use...	Avoid...
find	locate, identify
help	assist
make sure, confirm	verify, validate
message	prompt
put	incorporate
turn on	power on
use	utilize
voting machine	terminal

Revising. In these instructions from a poll worker's guide, the first step uses computer and election terminology (election definition, card, operating system, LCD screen) and includes more information than the poll workers need.

Before

1. Insert the scanner key and turn it to the Open/Close Poll position.

   It will take approximately two minutes for the scanner to load the election definition from the card into its operating system. The scanner will display "S-Mode" in the upper left corner of the LCD screen and the message "Election card inserted. Open polls now?"

2. Press Yes.

After

1. Insert the scanner key and turn it to Open/Close Poll.

2. Wait until this message appears (in about two minutes):

   Election card inserted. Open polls now?

3. Press Yes.

Why? Familiar, common words are easier to understand and remember. All users benefit from documentation that uses simple words, especially poll workers.

Evaluation checklist

☐ Does the documentation use words the users understand?

☐ Does the documentation use short, simple words?

☐ Does the documentation avoid unfamiliar election jargon?

☐ Does the documentation avoid computer and software terminology?

☐ Are unfamiliar terms explained when they appear?

☐ Does poll worker documentation avoid acronyms and abbreviations?

☐ Are acronyms and abbreviations defined when they appear?

Use consistent terminology

Use the same word consistently to describe a particular object or action.

What? Using consistent terminology means using the same word or phrase to describe a particular object or action each time it appears in the documentation in text, headings, captions, and graphics, as well as in printed reports, messages on screen, and labels on voting equipment.

How?

- Pick one term to use for a particular action or object.

- Create a terminology table to keep track of preferred words and (unused) alternatives.

- Replace the alternatives in the documentation with the preferred word.

- Work with the voting equipment developers to agree on terminology.

Revising. In this poll worker's guide, the text and the caption for the graphic use different terms: two terms for the object (roll and printer tape) and two for the action (feeds and rolls out). It is especially confusing that a single word (roll) is used for both the object and the action.

Before

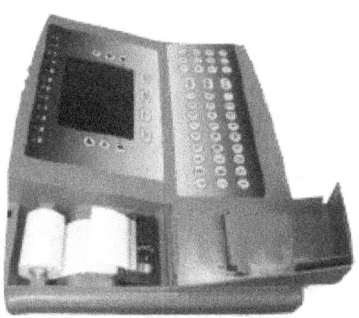

1. Insert the new roll so that it feeds from the bottom.

Printer tape rolls out from bottom

After

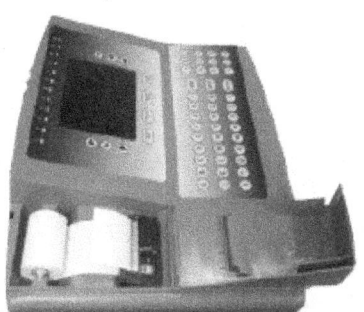

1. Insert the new roll so that it feeds from the bottom.

New roll feeds from bottom

Why? Users may be confused if the same object has different names or the same action is described in different terms. They may think that the documentation is discussing different objects or actions.

Evaluation checklist

☐ Is terminology consistent in text, headings, captions, and graphics?

☐ Is the terminology in the documentation consistent with the hardware and user interface terminology?

Tip! Don't use synonyms just to make your writing more interesting. They may also make it more difficult to read and understand.

Use gender neutral language

When you refer to both men and women, use words that refer to both. Don't use gender-based pronouns or words that refer to only one gender.

What? Gender-based pronouns refer to only one gender (male or female): she, her, hers, he, his, and so on. They are appropriate when you to refer a particular person.

How?

- Rewrite sentences in the plural to avoid gender-based pronouns.

- Use nouns instead of gender-based pronouns.

- Use articles instead of gender-based pronouns.

- Avoid using "one" and "he or she" or "he/she."

Good examples. These sentences use "their" and "a" rather than "his."

All voters who are in line before the polls close can cast their ballots.

Any voter who is in line before the polls close can cast a ballot.

Another good example. This sentence uses "the person's."

To vote for a write-in candidate, write the person's name on the line.

Revising. The steps explain how to assist a voter. They include seven gender-based pronouns. The revision replaces three of the pronouns with the noun, "the voter," and two with "the." It eliminates the need for the other two pronouns.

Before

1. Show him the keypad, and show him where to insert his ballot.

2. Assist him while he inserts his ballot for scanning (if he asks for assistance).

After

1. Show the voter the keypad and where to insert the ballot.

2. Assist the voter with inserting the ballot for scanning (if the voter asks for assistance).

Why? A gender-based pronoun can give the impression that the members of the other gender are not included.

Evaluation checklist

☐ Does the documentation avoid using gender-based pronouns?

Writing directly to your users

When documentation does not speak directly to users and tell them what to do, they mentally rephrase the information to create a scenario they can follow.

When the documentation speaks directly to users and clearly tells them what to do, they can spend more time working and less time reading.

To write directly to your users:

- Use the imperative in instructions
- Use "you" when writing to your users
- Use the active voice

Use the imperative in instructions

Use the imperative to tell your users what to do.

What? In the imperative, the subject of the sentence is "you," implied or understood, rather than stated directly. (For example: Open the panel.)

How? Use the imperative to:

- Tell your users what to do rather than describe what they do.
- Tell your users how to use voting equipment rather than describe it.

Good examples. These instructions tell poll workers exactly what to do.

Raise the switch cover.

Enter the Polling Place I.D.

Tear off the Open Polls report and file it in the appropriate envelope.

Revising. The poll workers must complete this action, but the step doesn't tell them that. The subject is the equipment, not "you" implied.

Before

1. The panel must be opened to remove the ballot.

After

1. Open the panel.
2. Remove the ballot.

More revising. This step from a poll worker's guide describes the equipment, not what the poll workers need to do.

Before

1. After the roller guide has been removed, it may be put back with the rollers down for long ballots or up for short ballots.

After

1. Remove the roller guide.
2. Put the roller guide back with the rollers down for long ballots or up for short ballots.

Why? Instructions that are written in the imperative are easier for users to understand. Instructions tell users what to do. Writing instructions in the imperative is the most direct way to do that.

Evaluation checklist

☐ Are instructions written in the imperative?

Use "you" when writing to your users

Refer to the assumed readers of the documentation as "you."

What? In a sentence that speaks directly to your users, the subject is the pronoun "you," either stated (You remove the seal) or implied (Remove the seal).

How?

- When discussing a condition or situation, use "you" to write to the users rather than referring to them in the third person, for example, as "the poll workers" in a poll worker's guide.

- When discussing voting equipment, use "you" to write to your users rather than describing the equipment.

See also

- Use the imperative in instructions (page 29)

Good examples. The sentence, heading, and note from a poll worker's guide speak directly to poll workers as "you."

> This training guide will provide you with the instructions for setting up the voting equipment in a polling place.

> Chapter 1: Before You Begin

> Note: You can write Election Keys with the poll status of the Judge's Check-In Station either "open" or "closed."

Revising. This sentence from a poll worker's guide explains why the voting machine must be locked. Poll workers must complete this action, but the sentence does not tell them that. It describes the equipment.

> **Before**
> After the polls have closed and all ballots counted, the voting machine must be electronically locked prevent further ballot counting and to issue the election tally.

> **After**
> After you have closed the polls and counted all ballots, you must electronically lock the voting machine to prevent further ballot counting and to issue the election tally.

More revising. This sentence from a troubleshooting guide talks about the equipment and poll workers. It doesn't tell them what to do.

Before

Poll workers should make sure the unit is on. The ballot box should be unlocked and opened. Poll workers should then make sure the power cord is plugged into the back of the unit.

After

1. Make sure the unit is on.

2. Unlock and open the ballot box.

3. Make sure the power cord is plugged into the back of the unit.

Why? When the documentation speaks directly to the users, they understand more quickly that they are the ones who should take action or perform a task. When the documentation describes the equipment, users need to figure out what action is required and who should do it.

Evaluation checklist

☐ Does the documentation use "you" to write directly to the users rather than referring to them in the third person?

☐ Does the documentation use "you" to write directly to the users rather than describing the equipment?

Tip! You can use "we" to speak as the voting system manufacturer. For example, "We recommend that you check the power connection often."

Use the active voice

Write sentences in the active voice most of the time. Use the passive voice only when necessary.

What? A sentence in English can be in either active or passive voice.

Active sentences have this pattern: actor — action — object.

> You will file the report at the end of Election Day.

> The voting machine records the ballot.

Passive sentences have this pattern: object — action — by the actor. Often, the actor is omitted.

> The report will be filed at the end of Election Day.

> The ballot is recorded.

An imperative sentence has this pattern: you — action — object. It is always active.

> Remove the ballot.

> Lock the panel.

How?

- Make the actors (your users) the subjects of your sentences, rather than the voting equipment.

See also

- Use the imperative in instructions (page 29)

- Use "you" when writing to your users (page 30)

Note: The passive voice is appropriate when it doesn't matter who the actor is or when you want your users to focus on the object. For example: Make sure that the cord is plugged in. The users don't know who plugged in the cord (or may have failed to), but it doesn't matter.

Revising. The sentence from a poll worker's guide explains how to prevent paper jams, but it doesn't tell the poll workers that they may need to do it. It describes the equipment.

Before

The Roller Guide allows the printer to be configured for various ballot lengths. It must be configured appropriately to prevent paper jams.

After

To prevent paper jams, you may need to configure the Roller Guide for the appropriate ballot length.

Why? Most readers understand sentences in the active voice more easily and quickly. Sentences in the active voice are also usually shorter and more direct.

Evaluation checklist

☐ Are most sentences in the active voice (and in passive only when appropriate)?

Keeping instructions short and simple

Most readers find short sentences (and short steps in instructions) easier to understand.

People can process only a limited amount of information at a time. Short steps break larger procedures down into manageable chunks of information. Short steps help limit how much users need to think about at one time.

But being short is not in itself enough to make a step easy to understand. The order of the words, phrases, and clauses in a step also affects comprehension. Steps that are grammatically simple, with the important information in the main clause, are easier for users to follow.

To keep instructions short and simple:

- Make each instruction a separate step
- Use numbers for steps
- Use bullets for lists
- Put steps in the order in which they must be completed
- Put information in a step in the order needed
- Put warnings before—not after—consequences
- Make each step as short as possible

Make each instruction a separate step

Make each action a new step and start each step on a new line.

What? A step is a single action. Users read a step and then complete the action, usually by turning away from the instructions.

How? Break each task down into a series of actions and then make each action a step.

Good example. Each action is a new step.

1. Place the unit on a table with the bottom storage side facing up.

2. Turn the four latches to a 45-degree angle.

3. Remove the bottom storage cover.

4. Remove the legs.

5. Replace the bottom storage cover.

6. Turn the latches to the original locked position.

Another good example. In a poll worker's guide, a single step in a long procedure is broken down into a series of actions. Each action starts on a new line.

1. When a voter needs to use curbside voting:

   a. Qualify the voter.

   b. Ask for the voter's preferred language.

   c. Ask if the voter needs tactile input switches or headphones.

   d. Assign an Access Code as usual.

Revising. One step with three actions becomes three steps. The phrase "When finished" isn't necessary when the actions are numbered steps.

Before

1. On the back of the voting unit, find the power receptacle (AC In). Plug the power cord into power receptacle (AC In). When finished, store the top cover in a safe location.

After

1. On the back of the voting unit, find the power receptacle (AC In).

2. Plug the power cord into the power receptacle (AC In).

3. Store the top cover in a safe location.

Why? Most users take the first reasonable action they come to. When each action is a new step, users can:

- Find their place in the instructions when they switch their attention (for example, from the instructions, to the voting system or voter, and then back to the instructions).

- See that there are multiple actions that they need to take.

- See all the instructions and avoid missing any.

Exception. A step can contain short, closely related actions. But users must be able to complete the actions without rereading the step.

For example:

Tear off the report and file it in the appropriate envelope.

Lift the unit, turn it right side up, and set it on the floor.

Evaluation checklist

☐ Is each action a new step?

☐ Does each step start on a new line?

☐ Are complex actions broken down into multiple steps if necessary?

☐ Exception. If a step contains more than one action, are the actions short and closely related?

Tip! Review the documentation for any steps that are more than a single line long to make sure that they cover only one action.

Use numbers for steps

Use numbers for the steps in instructions.

What? Instructions consist of numbered steps in the order in which they must be completed. Numbered steps tell users what to do.

How?

- Make each action the users take a step.

- Number each step.

- Do not use bullets instead of numbers for steps.

- Do not use numbered lists for anything other than steps.

- Do not number descriptions of system actions or changes.

Good examples. See the examples in "Make each instruction a separate step" on page 35.

Revising. The bullet list is actually a series of steps. The steps should be numbered rather than bulleted.

Before

- Insert the Supervisor card.

- Enter the password.

- Remove the Supervisor card.

After

1. Insert the Supervisor card.

2. Enter the password.

3. Remove the Supervisor card.

More revising. In this example from a poll worker's guide, the first step is an action that the poll workers take, but steps 2 and 3 are system actions. The poll workers' actions should be steps, not the system's actions.

Before

1. Turn the power on.

2. A password screen appears.

   To enter the password, you may use your stylus on the numeric on-screen keypad or the keys on the physical keypad. After entering the password, touch the green arrow.

3. After several moments, an Administration screen appears.

After

1. Turn the power on.

   A password screen appears.

2. To enter the password, use your stylus on the numeric on-screen keypad or the keys on the physical keypad.

3. Touch the green arrow.

   After several moments, an Administration screen appears.

Why? When steps are numbered, users can more easily:

- Skim and scan the documentation to find the instructions they need.

- Recognize instructions as a series of steps to follow.

- Find their place in instructions as they work through the steps.

- Avoid missing any steps.

Evaluation checklist

☐ Is each action that the users take a step?

☐ Is each step numbered?

☐ Are the steps in the order in which they must be completed?

☐ Are descriptions of system actions in instructions presented as paragraphs or notes rather than as numbered items?

Tip! Review bulleted lists in the documentation to make sure they are not really steps that should be numbered.

Use bullets for lists

Use bullets for all other lists that are not instructions.

What? Bulleted lists are lists of related items, with the most important or most frequently used items first.

How?

- Use bullets, not numbers, for lists of related items.

- Put the most important or most frequently used items first.

- Make the items grammatically parallel.

- Use vertical rather than horizontal lists.

Good example. This is a list from a poll worker's guide that tells the poll workers when they should cancel voting on an electronic voting booth. The items are parallel (all sentences) and the most likely is at the top.

Cancel voting on a booth if:

- A voter gets the wrong ballot style or language.

- A voter needs a unit with a different feature.

- A voter walks away from the booth with an active ballot.

Revising. This list of error messages is in the order of the most frequently used items, but it should be bulleted rather than numbered.

Before

1. Overvoted Race

2. Undervoted Race

3. Blank Voted Race

After

- Overvoted Race

- Undervoted Race

- Blank Voted Race

Why? Bulleted lists break up blocks of text and make skimming and scanning easier. When instructions are numbered and all other lists are bulleted, users can more easily tell the difference between the instructions and other information.

Note: Putting the most important or frequently used items first is important because readers tend to stop scanning a list as soon as they see something relevant.

Evaluation checklist

☐   Are bullets (not numbers) used for lists of related items?

☐   In bulleted lists, are the most important or most frequently used items first?

☐   Are the items in bulleted lists grammatically parallel?

Put steps in the order in which they must be completed

Put the first step first, the last step last—and all the steps in between in the order they occur.

What? Steps, comments, exceptions, and warnings appear in instructions in a linear order. Users tend to read information in instructions in the order it appears and attempt to follow it in that order.

How? In instructions:

- Put steps in the order users must complete them.

- Number the steps.

- Include other information at the point users need it to complete a step.

See also

- Organize the documentation logically and clearly (page 18)

Good example. In this poll worker's guide, the steps are in order and numbered (or lettered). The illustration appears when the poll workers need it. The comment about the screen display and note about the report appear when the poll workers see those system actions.

1. After the polls are closed, go to the back of the voting unit and complete these tasks:

    a. Break the seal on the Polls Open/Closed switch cover by twisting it.

    b. Place the broken seal in the Results bag.

    c. Lift up the cover and turn the Polls switch to Closed.

The screen displays the totals.

Note: The Official Election Results Report will begin to print.

2. Record the totals on the form.

Revising. In this example from a poll worker's guide, the preparation for transmitting is in step 1; the transmitting is in step 2. The poll workers need to prepare in step 1, but they don't need to know that the transmission starts until the end of the procedure.

Before

1. When you transmit results to election headquarters by modem, the scanner will begin to transmit after it has finished printing the reports. Unlock and open the Counter Access Panel, and connect the telephone cord to the modem jack below the scanner door.

2. Press Close Polls. The scanner will print the reports. After printing, if you transmit results, the scanner will begin to transmit automatically.

After

To transmit results to election headquarters by modem:

1. Unlock and open the Counter Access Panel.

2. Connect the telephone cord to the modem jack below the scanner door.

3. Press Close Polls.

   The scanner prints the reports and then transmits the results.

Why? Information that is presented in a logical order is easier to understand. This is especially true for series of steps in a procedure. When the steps are order, users can:

- Avoid missing important steps.

- Concentrate on the current step and forget the previous one.

- Save the time and effort of figuring out what to do next.

Evaluation checklist

☐ Are the steps in the order in which they must be completed?

☐ Are the steps numbered?

☐ Is other information included at the point the users need it to complete the steps?

Put information in a step in the order needed

Put information in each step in the order the users need it.

What? Some steps include phrases that explain where or how to complete an action or how long to continue it. Users need the information in the order they act on it.

How?

- Put information in the order users need it to do the task.

- Put the context before the action.

- Put the result after the action, unless it is a warning.

See also

- Put warnings before—not after—consequences (page 45)

Good examples

Each step is a single action, but it includes other information (emphasized with italics) in the order the users need it.

After the report prints, turn the key back to Vote.

Press and hold the black button *until the green light comes on.*

On the Polls Open Menu, press Add Voter.

The context (emphasized with italics) is before the action.

If the battery does not work, call the Help Desk.

To add a new voter, press Add Voter.

In a single step, the context is before the action and the information is in the order the users need it.

To add a new voter, on the Polls Open Menu, press Add Voter.

Revising. In this example, poll workers need to know where the Print button is before they can press it. They need to know why to select Yes or No before they do. The report prints before the message appears.

Before

1. Press the Print button on the scanner.

   The message "Print Another Report?" appears after the report prints.

   - Select Yes if you need another report.

   - Select No if you are finished with reports.

After

1. On the scanner, press the Print button.

   After the report prints, the message "Print Another Report?" appears.

2. Select one of the following:

   - If you need another report, select Yes.

   - If you are finished with reports, select No.

Why?

- Information that is presented in a logical order is easier to understand.

- When context comes before the action people can understand what the task is before they act.

- When the action comes before the context, people tend to act before they read the rest of the sentence, and so make more mistakes.

Evaluation checklist

☐ In each step, is the information in the order users need it to complete the task?

☐ In each step, is the context before the action?

☐ In each step, is the result after the action (unless it is a warning)?

Put warnings before—not after—consequences

Put warnings immediately before their consequences, not after or all together at the beginning of a guide or section.

What? Warnings tell users when something they do can cause harm to the voters, the voting process, or themselves. Users need to know what can happen before they take the action, not after.

How?

- Put warnings immediately before the step that can lead to a harmful consequence.

- Make sure the warning is on the same page as the related step.

- Repeat warnings for each step that can lead to a harmful consequence, not just the first relevant step in a procedure.

- If you put all the warnings at the beginning of a document, repeat them before each step that can lead to a harmful consequence.

- Make warnings stand out from the rest of the text, for example, with bold or italics or a small graphic.

- Put warnings in mixed case, not all capital letters.

Note: We recommend putting the signal word (for example, Warning) in mixed case, but people are also used to seeing it in all caps (WARNING).

Good example. The warning about where to plug in the cord comes immediately before the step to plug it in.

1. Plug the end of the power cord with the socket into the back of the scanner.

   Warning! Only plug the scanner into a grounded, three-pronged electrical outlet. Plug only one scanner into an outlet. Do not use an extension cord.

2. Plug the other end of the cord into a wall outlet.

Revising. The battery may explode before users find out it can.

Before

The Lithium-Ion Battery Pack can be replaced only by Authorized Service Personnel.

CAUTION: RISK OF EXPLOSION. THE BATTERY CAN EXPLODE IF IT IS REPLACED BY AN INCORRECT TYPE.

After

Caution! Risk of explosion! The battery can explode if it is replaced by an incorrect type.

The Lithium-Ion Battery Pack can be replaced only by Authorized Service Personnel.

More revising. In this poll worker's guide, the message appears before the poll workers look back to the instructions for the next step.

Before

1. Enter the password.

   The message "Clear Election Day Totals" appears.

2. **CAUTION!** Press No.

   Pressing Yes will cause the election results to be erased.

After

1. Enter the password.

2. **Caution!** Press No when the message "Clear Election Day Totals" appears.

   The election results will be erased if you press Yes.

Or

Caution! After you enter the password, the message "Clear Election Day Totals" will appear. Answer No.

The election results will be erased if you press Yes.

1. Enter the password.

2. Press No when the message "Clear Election Day Totals" appears.

Why? People often act as soon as they see an instruction. They need to know the consequences before it is too late.

Evaluation checklist

☐ Do warnings come immediately before harmful consequences?

☐ Are warnings on the same page as the harmful consequences?

☐ Are warnings in mixed case, not all capital letters?

☐ Do warnings stand out from the rest of the text?

Tip! Review the documentation for warnings and cautions to make sure they are immediately before the relevant step and on the same page.

Make each step as short as possible

What? A step consists of a brief action statement (or perhaps two short, closely related action statements). Some steps contain a brief sentence that explains how the system responds to the action (feedback).

How?

- Delete unnecessary words.

- Consider putting feedback from the system in a comment or note below the step.

See also

- Make each instruction a separate step (page 35)

- Use the imperative in instructions (page 29)

- Use familiar, common words (page 23)

- Put steps in the order in which they must be completed (page 41)

- Address one group of users at a time (page 13)

Good example. This complicated task from a poll worker's guide is a series of short steps. Feedback from the card activator is included after each step.

1. Push the voter card—arrow facing down—into the card activator slot until it clicks into place.

   The message **Activate this card?** appears.

2. Press the number **0**.

   The message **Provisional Voter?** appears.

3. Press the yellow **Yes** button.

   The message **Copy ID, then Press Yes** appears.

4. Copy the ID from the card activator to the provisional voter's form.

5. Press the yellow **Yes** button.

Revising. In this poll worker's guide, a single step contains several actions. It is written as a statement rather than in the imperative. It uses complex words, rather than simple, common ones. The information is not in the order that poll workers need it. The poll workers need to know that the voter can cast an overvoted ballot before they spoil that ballot.

Before

1. If an overvoted ballot is encountered, the voter should be provided with an alternate ballot, and instructed to mark the ballot without incurring an overvote, then return the ballot for processing. The overvoted ballot should be filed as spoiled. If the voter does not want to mark another ballot, and is content with the candidate selections on the original ballot, the overvoted ballot should be fed into the unit in override mode.

After

If an Overvoted Ballot message appears:

1. Explain overvoting to the voter.

2. Ask if the voter wants to mark a new ballot or turn in the overvoted ballot.

    -   If the voter wants to mark a new ballot:

        a. Give the voter a new ballot.

        b. File the overvoted ballot as spoiled.

    -   If the voter does not want to mark a new ballot:

        a. Ask the voter to put the overvoted ballot into the unit.

        b. Press the override button.

Why? Short steps are usually easier to read, understand, and remember.

Evaluation checklist

☐   Is each step as short as possible?

Tip! Review the documentation for any steps that are more than a single line long and determine if they can be shorter.

Using graphics effectively

People like graphics—photographs, illustrations, line drawings, all kinds of images. And graphics, especially along with text, help people understand what they read.

Graphics can help users understand how to use voting equipment. When the picture, the equipment, and perhaps their own visualization are the same, users can see where to work on the equipment and what to do.

To use graphics effectively:

- Use graphics to illustrate tasks
- Make the relationship between graphics and text clear
- Keep graphics simple—show only what is necessary
- Identify items and actions on graphics

Use graphics to illustrate tasks

Use illustrations, photographs, tables, charts, and other graphics whenever possible and appropriate.

What? Graphics include illustrations, photographs, flowcharts, tables, screenshots, icons, and so on.

How?

- When tasks involve voting equipment, use illustrations and photographs to show both the equipment and the actions to take.

- Use flowcharts to show a sequence of tasks, for example, the interaction of voters with different clerks and other poll workers on Election Day or the voters' path through the polling place.

- Use screenshots to show buttons, text boxes, and other screen elements for tasks.

Good example. The illustration of the LCD screen shows the area to check. The icon indicates that it's important.

6. Check AC and Batt (battery power) at the bottom of the screen.

   Both should say OKAY.

Another good example. The illustration shows where to press the brace.

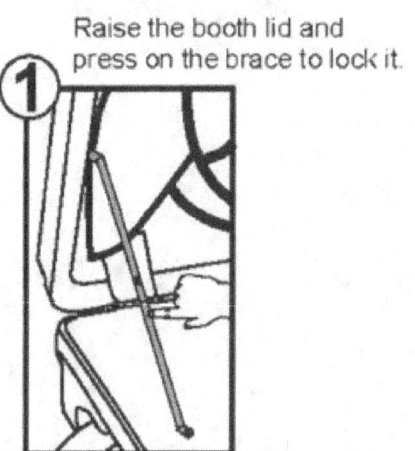

Raise the booth lid and press on the brace to lock it.

Why? Instructions that include text and pictures are more effective than instructions with text or pictures alone. Graphics can help users:

- Understand a task faster.

- Locate items on a screen or on a piece of equipment.

- Figure out how to complete complex physical tasks.

- Remember the instructions while they complete a task.

- Switch from the instructions to the task and back.

- Confirm where they are in a procedure.

- Confirm that they are doing steps in a task correctly.

Evaluation checklist

- ☐ Do illustrations or photographs show how to complete tasks that involve physical equipment?

- ☐ Do screenshots show what to look for or how to complete tasks that involve computer monitors?

- ☐ Do illustrations or photographs show what to look for or how to complete tasks that involve LCD screens?

Tip! Use tables to display closely related sets of information in a smaller space; for example, use a table for error messages to show in one line the message, the cause, and the solution.

Make the relationship between graphics and text clear

Put each graphic near the step it relates to and make the relationship between the graphic and the step clear.

What? Graphics and text together show how to complete a task. Users need to easily grasp how the two work together.

How?

- Put graphics near the appropriate step (next to or immediately after).

- Use consistent terminology between the graphic and step.

- Make the title of the graphic match the task in the step.

- If the placement of the graphic doesn't make the relationship with the step clear, explain it in the step with a reference to the graphic.

- Be as consistent as possible in the placement of graphics, but base it on explaining the task, not on creating a consistent or pleasing layout.

Good example. In this poll worker's guide, the graphics for steps 2 and 3 appear next to the steps that they relate to. (A blank space appears next to step 1 because it is not illustrated.) The terminology is consistent in the text and the graphics (Close Polls, close the polls).

1. Wait for all voters in the polling place to finish voting.

2. On the controller, press CLOSE POLLS. It is located below the screen.

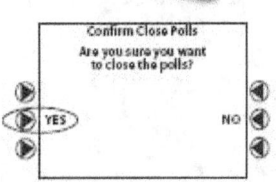

The controller confirms that you want to close the polls.

3. Press the button next to YES.

Another good example. In this poll worker's guide, the graphic appears next to the warning.

The official Zero Proof Report begins printing.

Do not remove the official zero proof report from the printer.

Revising. In this poll worker's guide, five steps appear next to one picture. Poll workers need to know which step goes with the picture.

Before

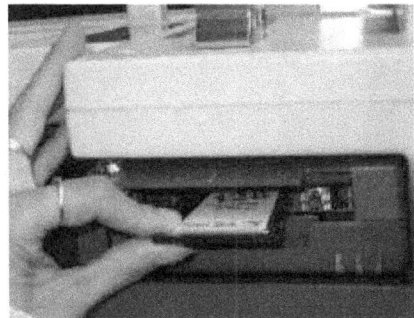

Remove the memory card

1. Disconnect the cable from the transfer compartment.
2. Close and lock the transfer compartment.
3. Unlock and open the data compartment.
4. Turn the unit off.
5. Remove the memory card from the data compartment.

After

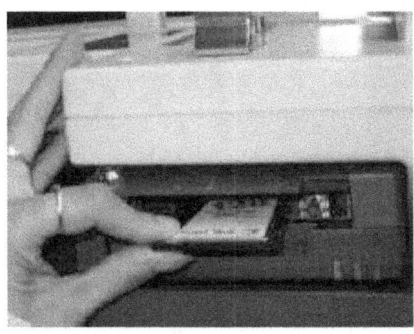

Remove the memory card

5. Remove the memory card from the data compartment.

Why? Instructions that include text and pictures are easier to read and understand, but only if users can easily see the relationship between the graphics and text.

Evaluation checklist

☐ Are the graphics near the appropriate steps?

☐ Is the terminology consistent between the graphics and the steps?

☐ Do the titles of the graphics match the tasks in the steps?

☐ If placement doesn't make the relationship between a graphic and a step clear, does the step explain it with a reference to the graphic?

Keep graphics simple—show only what is necessary

Show only what your users need to know, not the voting equipment in complete and perfect detail.

What? Simple graphics include a limited amount of information. Users need simple graphics so that they can quickly pick out the relevant information and determine what to do.

How?

- Include only what is necessary in illustrations and photographs for your users to complete their tasks.

- Show only the part of the voting equipment that is necessary for your users to complete their tasks (not the whole thing).

- Reduce visual noise by removing extraneous details.

- Focus on the actions your users should take (not the features of the equipment or interface).

- Use illustrations such as line drawings when photographs include too much information.

Good example. In this poll worker's guide, the photograph shows only the part of the voting booth leg that poll workers work with in this step.

1. To secure the leg brace, connect the upper and lower portions in the center.

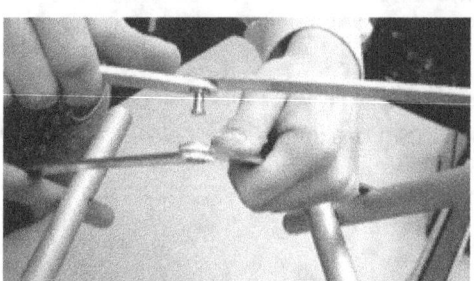

Revising. In this poll worker's guide, the photograph shows three complete units rather than just the part the poll workers need to understand, as well as bookshelves, tables, and other distractions.

Before

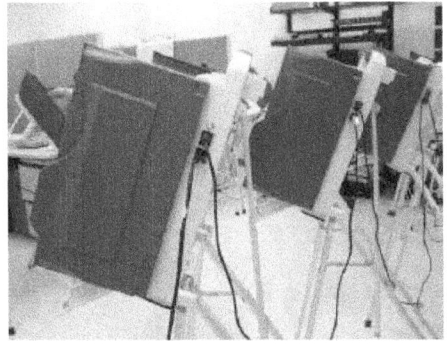

Daisy-chained units

1. Connect the unit to the power receptacle (AC in) of the previous unit.

   This creates a daisy-chain of the voting units.

After

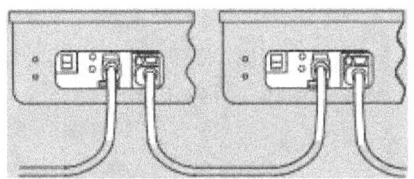

Daisy-chained units

1. Connect the unit to the power receptacle (AC in) of previous unit.

   This creates a daisy-chain of the voting units.

Why? Simple graphics help users focus on the appropriate areas of the visual description so they can read and understand them faster and more easily.

Evaluation checklist

☐ Are illustrations and photographs as simple as they can be?

☐ Do illustrations and photographs include only what is necessary for users to complete their tasks?

☐ Do graphics of voting equipment show only the parts necessary for users to complete their tasks?

☐ Do graphics focus on the actions users should take rather than the features of the equipment or interface?

Tip! Review the documentation for large, complicated "overview" graphics and replace these with smaller, simpler graphics at the appropriate step.

Identify items and actions on graphics

Use captions to identify the important parts of graphics and arrows to show the direction of action.

What? Captions, labels, and arrows identify specific areas on graphics. Arrows and other devices indicate the direction of the action.

How?

- Use labels and callouts to emphasize the important parts of graphics.

- Use arrows or other markings to indicate the direction of the action.

- Use captions to identify the main point of the graphic.

- Provide more information than users can get by simply looking at the actual voting equipment or screen.

See also

- Keep graphics simple—show only what is necessary (page 54)

Good example. The illustration shows only the part of the voting booth involved in the action. The step is the caption. The arrow points out the clip and shows the direction of the action.

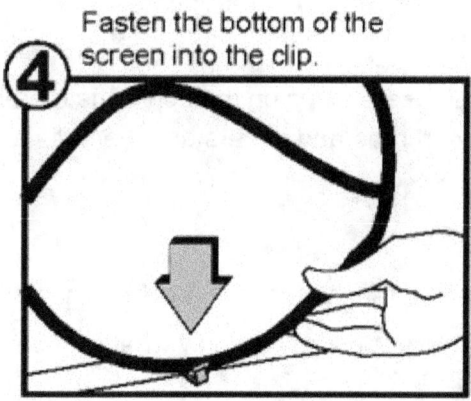

Fasten the bottom of the
screen into the clip.

Revising. The overview graphic labels the PC Card Slot, but it is difficult to pick out. The revision shows only the relevant part and the action. The caption describes the action.

Before

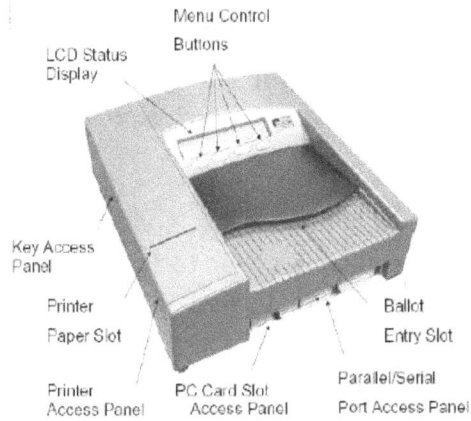

1. Insert the PC card into either slot.

   If one slot does not accept the card, try the other.

After

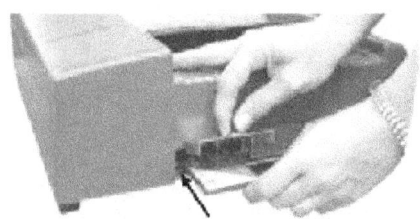

Insert PC card

1. Insert the PC card into either slot.

   If one slot does not accept the card, try the other.

Why? Users may focus on the biggest or brightest part of the illustration whether it is relevant on not. Labels and action indicators help users focus on the appropriate areas of a graphic and quickly find where to perform the action.

Evaluation checklist

☐ Are the important parts of graphics emphasized with labels or callouts?

☐ In graphics, is the direction of action shown with arrows or other markings?

☐ In graphics, is the main point identified with a caption?

☐ Do graphics provide more information than users can get by simply looking at the actual voting equipment or screen?

Designing the documentation for easy scanning and reading

Users scan documentation until they find what they need, rather than reading carefully from cover to cover.

For example, poll workers on Election Day use the poll workers' guide when they need to complete an unfamiliar task or solve a problem. They scan until they find what they need and then read. They want to get back to work as quickly as possible.

Headers and footers, headings, page numbers, a table of contents, and other navigation aids help users move through the documentation to find what they need. These aids also provide a context that helps users understand new information. The overall design of the page can also make scanning, as well as reading, easier.

To design the documentation for easy scanning and reading:

- Use informative headers and footers
- Design pages for easy scanning and reading

Use informative headers and footers

Show the page topic and the page number in the headers or footers.

What? Headers provide information about a page at the top of the page and footers provide information at the bottom.

How? Include this information in the headers or footers:

- Page topic (usually the chapter or section title)
- Page numbers
- If the documentation set includes more than one document, the document title

Good examples. These page headers show the subjects of the page.

setting up: removing booths from storage caddy

opening polls for election day

curbside voting

The footer shows the page number and the title of the guide.

D E S K R E F E R E N C E

10

Note: Although headers and footers normally use either sentence or title capitalization (for example, Setting up or Setting Up), this example uses other typographic devices effectively.

Why? Informative headers and footers help users scan the documentation and find their way through it quickly.

Evaluation checklist

☐ Do the headers show the page topic (chapter or section title)?

☐ Do the headers or footers show the page numbers?

☐ If the documentation set includes more than one document, do the headers or footers show the document title?

Design pages for easy scanning and reading

Design pages that your users can scan quickly and read easily. Use appropriate font size, leading, line length, and layout.

What? Page design includes layout, typography (font size, leading, and line length), type face, techniques for emphasizing, text alignment, and more.

How?

- Use familiar fonts (either serif or sans serif or both).
- Use a legible font size (about 12 points for text).
- Use font variations consistently, for example, in headings and captions.
- Use appropriate leading; that is, space between lines (1 to 4 points).
- Use a reasonable line length (8 or 9 words a line).
- Use mixed case (not all caps) for the text.
- Use emphasis to highlight important information (but don't overdo it).
- Use bold or italics rather than all caps to show emphasis.
- Use a physical format suitable for the work place.

Examples

This guide uses:

- A sans serif font (Arial)
- 11 point type
- Leading of 11/15 or 4 points (11 point type with 15 point line spacing)
- A line length that may be slightly too long for optimal reading, about 10 or 11 words
- Mixed case for text and headings
- Italics for *emphasis*
- PDF with a page size of 8½ by 11 inches for delivery

This guide does *not* use:

- An unfamiliar font like Gill Sans MT or AmericanaT
- 10 point type or 8 point type or 14 point type for text
- ALL CAPS FOR TEXT, HEADINGS, OR EMPHASIS

Why? Readers find familiar fonts, mixed case, bigger fonts (12 point), and shorter lines easier to read. These elements help users skim for information more quickly and read it more easily.

Evaluation checklist

☐ Are the fonts familiar?

☐ Is the font size legible (about 12 pt)?

☐ Are font variations consistent, for example, in headings and captions?

☐ Is the leading appropriate (1 to 4 points)?

☐ Are the lines a reasonable length (8 or 9 words a line)?

☐ Is mixed case rather than all caps used for the text?

☐ Is important information highlighted with bold or italics?

☐ Is the physical format of the documentation suitable for the work place?

Tip! If you don't have someone with graphic design skills on your team, consider hiring a consultant to help with your page design.

Testing the documentation

Test the documentation throughout development to make sure people can use it to complete their tasks.

What? Testing documentation means having someone use it to complete a task while you watch to see if the documentation helps them do that easily, and then revising the documentation based on what you learn.

How?

- Observe other people following instructions you have written. Watch without training, helping, or hinting.

- Take notes about where people had problems following the instructions or made mistakes.

- Test throughout the development cycle, starting at the beginning, not just at the end.

- Use what you learn to revise the documentation and then test again.

- Do informal try-outs as often as possible.

- Do at least one formal usability test with your users or participants like your users.

- Test the documentation yourself often by doing tasks as if you were one of the personas you created. (See "Understand your users" page 9.) But don't rely solely on these tests!

- For more about usability testing, see the resources on page 69.

Why? You are not your user, so you cannot imagine how well the documentation will work. Even if you are a poll worker, you experience only one part of the election process in one polling place, not the full variety other people involved in the election process may face. Testing the documentation can help you discover and correct problems that you overlooked so your users don't encounter them during the election process—especially on Election Day.

Evaluation checklist

- ☐ Is the document easy for people to use to do their job throughout the election process and especially on Election Day?

Tip! If you don't have someone with experience in usability testing on your team, consider hiring a consultant to help you design your ongoing informal try-outs and formal usability test.

Checklist

Writing the documentation for specific users
Address one group of users at a time

☐ Does the documentation address one group of users at a time?

☐ Does each document or major section include only the information needed by the group of users it addresses?

☐ Is the poll worker's guide a separate document rather than a chapter in a multipurpose guide?

☐ Does the poll worker's guide include only the information that poll workers need?

Organizing to meet your users' needs
Focus on your users' tasks

☐ Does the documentation explain how to complete the tasks rather than describe the voting equipment?

☐ Is voting equipment explained with the tasks, rather than in overviews?

Organize the documentation logically and clearly

☐ Is the documentation organized logically based on the user's tasks?

☐ If the users must complete the tasks in a particular order, is the document organized chronologically based on that order?

☐ When chronological order is not important, is the document organized by the importance or frequency of the tasks?

☐ Is the poll worker's guide in particular organized chronologically based on the poll workers' tasks?

Use informative headings

☐ Do the headings describe users' tasks rather than equipment?

☐ Are the headings in an effective form: verbs, questions, or sentences?

☐ Are the headings in a section grammatically parallel?

Using simple words your users understand
Use familiar, common words

☐ Does the documentation use words the users understand?

☐ Does the documentation use short, simple words?

☐ Does the documentation avoid unfamiliar election jargon?

☐ Does the documentation avoid computer and software terminology?

☐ Are unfamiliar terms explained when they appear?

☐ Does poll worker documentation avoid acronyms and abbreviations?

☐ Are acronyms and abbreviations defined when they appear?

Use consistent terminology

☐ Is terminology consistent in text, headings, captions, and graphics?

☐ Is the terminology in the documentation consistent with the hardware and user interface terminology?

Use gender neutral language

☐ Does the documentation avoid using gender-based pronouns?

Writing directly to your users

Use the imperative in instructions

☐ Are instructions written in the imperative?

Use "you" when writing to your users

☐ Does the documentation use "you" to write directly to the users rather than referring to them in the third person?

☐ Does the documentation use "you" to write directly to the users rather than describing the equipment?

Use the active voice

☐ Are most sentences in the active voice (and in passive only when appropriate)?

Keeping instructions short and simple

Make each instruction a separate step

☐ Is each action a new step?

☐ Does each step start on a new line?

☐ Are complex actions broken down into multiple steps if necessary?

☐ Exception. If a step contains more than one action, are the actions short and closely related?

Use numbers for steps

☐ Is each action that the users take a step?

☐ Is each step numbered?

☐ Are the steps in the order in which they must be completed?

☐ Are descriptions of system actions in instructions presented as paragraphs or notes rather than as numbered items?

Use bullets for lists

☐ Are bullets (not numbers) used for lists of related items?

☐ In bulleted lists, are the most important or most frequently used items first?

☐ Are the items in bulleted lists grammatically parallel?

Put steps in the order in which they must be completed

☐ Are the steps in the order in which they must be completed?

☐ Are the steps numbered?

☐ Is other information included at the point the users need it to complete the steps?

Put information in a step in the order needed

☐ In each step, is the information in the order users need it to complete the task?

☐ In each step, is the context before the action?

☐ In each step, is the result after the action (unless it is a warning)?

Put warnings before—not after—consequences

☐ Do warnings come immediately before harmful consequences?

☐ Are warnings on the same page as the harmful consequences?

☐ Are warnings in mixed case, not all capital letters?

☐ Do warnings stand out from the rest of the text?

Make each step as short as possible

☐ Is each step as short as possible?

Using graphics

Use graphics to illustrate tasks

☐ Do illustrations or photographs show how to complete tasks that involve physical equipment?

☐ Do screenshots show what to look for or how to complete tasks that involve computer monitors?

☐ Do illustrations or photographs show what to look for or how to complete tasks that involve LCD screens?

Make the relationship between graphics and text clear

☐ Are the graphics near the appropriate steps?

☐ Is the terminology consistent between the graphics and the steps?

☐ Do the titles of the graphics match the tasks in the steps?

☐ If placement doesn't make the relationship between a graphic and a step clear, does the step explain it with a reference to the graphic?

Keep graphics simple—show only what is necessary

- ☐ Are illustrations and photographs as simple as they can be?
- ☐ Do illustrations and photographs include only what is necessary for users to complete their tasks?
- ☐ Do graphics of voting equipment show only the parts necessary for users to complete their tasks?
- ☐ Do graphics focus on the actions users should take rather than the features of the equipment or interface?

Identify items and actions on graphics

- ☐ Are the important parts of graphics emphasized with labels or callouts?
- ☐ In graphics, is the direction of action shown with arrows or other markings?
- ☐ In graphics, is the main point identified with a caption?
- ☐ Do graphics provide more information than users can get by simply looking at the actual voting equipment or screen?

Designing the documentation for easy scanning and reading

Use informative headers and footers

- ☐ Do the headers show the page topic (chapter or section title)?
- ☐ Do the headers or footers show the page numbers?
- ☐ If the documentation set includes more than one document, do the headers or footers show the document title?

Design pages for easy scanning and reading

- ☐ Are the fonts familiar?
- ☐ Is the font size legible (about 12 pt)?
- ☐ Are font variations consistent, for example, in headings and captions?
- ☐ Is the leading appropriate (1 to 4 points)?
- ☐ Are the lines a reasonable length (8 or 9 words a line)?
- ☐ Is mixed case rather than all caps used for the text?
- ☐ Is important information highlighted with bold or italics?
- ☐ Is the physical format of the documentation suitable for the work place?

Testing the documentation

- ☐ Is the document easy for people to use to do their job throughout the election process and especially on Election Day?

Resources

These books, web sites, and other resources provide more information on how to follow the guidelines. They are presented by section, but because the ideas are closely related, a resource listed in one category is often relevant to several others. Within a category, the resources are listed in the order that we have found them most helpful.

Writing the documentation for specific users

Resources on user-centered design and personas

User and Task Analysis for Interface Design by JoAnn T. Hackos and Janice C. Redish. New York, NY: John Wiley & Sons, 1998.

The User is Always Right: A Practical Guide to Creating and Using Personas for the Web by Steve Mulder with Ziv Yaar. Berkeley, CA: New Riders Press, 2006.

Understanding Your Users: A Practical Guide to User Requirements Methods, Tools, and Techniques by Catherine Courage and Kathy Baxter. San Francisco, CA: Morgan Kaufmann, 2004.

The Persona Lifecycle: Keeping People in Mind Throughout Product Design by John Pruitt and Tamara Adlin. San Francisco, CA: Morgan Kaufmann, 2006.

Organizing to meet your users' needs

Resources on information design and information architecture

Dynamics in Document Design by Karen A. Schriver. New York: John Wiley & Sons, 1997.

Minimalism beyond the Nurnberg Funnel by John M. Carroll, editor, and others. Cambridge, MA: The MIT Press, 1998.

Using simple words your users understand

Resources on plain language and writing clearly

PlainLanguage.gov. *Federal Plain Language Guidelines.* http://www.plainlanguage.gov.

Plain Talk. The State of Washington's *Plain Talk Guidelines.* http://www.accountability.wa.gov/plaintalk.

Usability.gov. *Research-Based Web Design & Usability Guidelines.* http://www.usability.gov/pdfs/guidelines.html.

Letting Go of the Words by Janice (Ginny) Redish. San Francisco: Morgan Kaufmann, 2007.

Writing directly to your users

See the resources for "Using simple words your users understand" on page 67.

Keeping instructions short and simple

Resources on writing instructions

Guidelines for Writing Clear Instructions and Messages for Voters and Poll Workers by Janice (Ginny) Redish. NIST, 2006. Available at: http://vote.nist.gov/032906PlainLanguageRpt.pdf

See also the resources for "Using simple words your users understand" on page 67.

Using graphics effectively

Resources on using graphics in documentation

Illustrating Computer Documentation: The Art of Presenting Information Graphically on Paper and Online by William Horton. New York: Wiley, 1991.

The Visual Display of Quantitative Information (Second Edition) by Edward R. Tufte. Cheshire, CT: Graphics Press, 2001.

Envisioning Information by Edward R. Tufte. Cheshire, CT: Graphics Press, 1990.

Visual Explanations: Images and Quantities, Evidence and Narrative by Edward R. Tufte. Cheshire, CT: Graphics Press, 1997.

See also: *Dynamics in Document Design* by Karen A. Schriver. New York, NY: John Wiley & Sons, 1997.

Designing the documentation for easy scanning and reading

Resources on document design

The Non-Designer's Design Book (3rd Edition) by Robin Williams. Berkeley, CA: Peachpit Press, 2008.

UI Design Newsletter. http://www.humanfactors.com

See also: *Dynamics in Document Design* by Karen A. Schriver. New York: John Wiley & Sons, 1997.

Testing the documentation
Resources on usability testing

A Practical Guide to Usability Testing by Joseph S. Dumas and Janice C. Redish. Intellect, 1999.

Handbook of Usability Testing by Jeff Rubin and Dana Chisnell. Indianapolis, IN: Wiley Publishing, Inc., 2008. In press.

Journal of Usability Studies.
http://www.usabilityprofessionals.org/upa_publications/jus/jus_home.html

References

References include those from the literature and guidelines reviews:

- *Review of relevant literature: technical communication and information design* (Chisnell and Becker 2007a)

- *Current guidelines: technical communication and information design* (Chisnell and Becker 2007b)

Alred, Gerald J. 2003. Essential works on technical communication. *Technical Communication* 50 (4): 585-616.

Arditi, Aries and Jianna Cho. 2005. Serifs and font legibility. *Vision Research* 45 (23): 2926-2933.

Bailey, Bob. 2000. Reducing reliance on superstition. *UI Design Newsletter*, September, http://www.humanfactors.com/downloads/sep00.asp# (accessed December 4, 2007).

Bailey, Bob. 2002a. More about fonts. *UI Design Newsletter*, February, http://www.humanfactors.com/downloads/feb02.asp (accessed December 6, 2007).

Bailey, Bob. 2002b. Optimal line length. *UI Design Newsletter*, November, http://www.humanfactors.com/downloads/nov02.asp (accessed December 6, 2007).

Baker, J. Ryan. 2005. Is multiple-column online text better? *Usability News* 7.2. http://psychology.wichita.edu/surl/usabilitynews/72/columns.htm (accessed December 12, 2007).

Bernard, Michael, Chia Hui Liao, and Melissa Mills. 2001. Effects of font type and size on the legibility and reading time of online text by older adults. Paper presented at ACM SIGCHI 2001. http://psychology.wichita.edu/surl/usabilitynews/3W/fontSR.htm (accessed December 12, 2007).

Blakeslee, Ann M., and Rachel Spilka. 2004. The state of research in technical communication. *Technical Communication Quarterly* 13 (1): 73-92.

Boekelder, Angelique, and Michael Steehouder. 1998. Selecting and switching: Some advantages of diagrams over tables and lists for presenting instructions. *IEEE Transactions on Professional Communication* 41 (4): 229-241.

Boekelder, Angelique, and Michael Steehouder. 1999. Switching from instructions to equipment: The effect of graphic design. In *Visual information for everyday use: Design and research perspectives*, ed. Harm J. G. Zwaga, Theo Boersema, and Henriette C. M. Hoonout, 67-73. London: Taylor and Francis.

Botka, Dana Howard. 2002. From gobbledygook to plain English: How a large state agency took on the bureaucratic form letter. In *Proceedings: STC's 49th Annual Conference.* Society for Technical Communication. http://www.stc.org/ConfProceed/2002/PDFs/STC49-00022.pdf (accessed October 15, 2007).

Brumberger, Eva R. 2003a. The rhetoric of typography: The awareness and impact of typeface appropriateness. *Technical Communication* 50 (2): 224-231.

Brumberger, Eva R. 2003b. The rhetoric of typography: The persona of typeface and text. *Technical Communication* 50 (2): 206-223.

Brumberger, Eva R. 2004. The rhetoric of typography: Effects on reading time, reading comprehension, and perceptions of ethos. *Technical Communication* 51 (1): 13-24.

Burton, Susan. 2007. You may already be a technical communicator! *Intercom*, June, 4.

Carliner, Saul. 2006. Current challenges of research in information and document design. In *Information and document design: Variety on the research*, ed. Saul Carliner, Jan Piet Verckens, and Cathy de Waele, 1-24. Amsterdam, The Netherlands: John Benjamins.

Carroll, John M. 1990. *The Nurnberg Funnel: Designing minimalist instruction for practical computer skill*. Cambridge, MA: MIT Press.

Carroll, John M., ed. 1998. *Minimalism beyond the Nurnberg Funnel*. Cambridge: The MIT Press.

Chisnell, Dana E., and Susan C. Becker. 2007a. *Review of relevant literature: technical communication and information design*. Working paper for National Institute of Standards and Technology (NIST).

Chisnell, Dana E., and Susan C. Becker. 2007b. *Current guidelines: technical communication and information design.* Working paper for National Institute of Standards and Technology (NIST).

Chisnell, Dana E., and Susan C. Becker. 2008a. *Gaps between voting system documentation and best practice in technical communication and information design.* Working paper for National Institute of Standards and Technology (NIST).

Chisnell, Dana E., and Susan C. Becker. 2008b. *Applying best practice in technical communication and information design to documentation for poll workers.* Working paper for National Institute of Standards and Technology (NIST).

Dixon, Peter. 1987. The processing of organizational and component step information in written directions. *Journal of Memory and Language* 6: 24-35.

Doumont, Jean-luc. 2002. Magical numbers: The seven-plus-or-minus-two myth. *IEEE Transactions on Professional Communication* 45 (2), 123-127.

Farkas, David K. 1999. The logical and rhetorical construction of procedural discourse. *Technical Communication* 46 (1): 42-54.

Felker, Daniel B., Marshall Atlas, Veda R. Charrow, V. Melissa Holland, Cheryl Olkes, Janice C. (Ginny) Redish, and Andrew M. Rose. 1980. *Document design: A review of the relevant research.* Washington, DC: American Institutes for Research.

Felker, Daniel B., Frances Pickering, Veda R. Charrow, V. Melissa Holland, and Janice C. (Ginny) Redish. 1981. *Guidelines for document designers.* Washington, DC: American Institutes for Research.

Ganier, Frank. 2004. Factors affecting the processing of procedural instructions: Implications for document design. *IEEE Transactions on Professional Communication* 47 (1): 15-26.

Garvery, Philip M., Martin T. Pietrucha, and Donald Meeker. 1997. Effects of font and capitalization on legibility of guide signs. *Transportation Research Record* 1605: 73-79. http://clearviewhwy.com/ResearchAndDesign/researchWhitepapers.php (accessed December 6, 2007).

Gellevij, Mark, and Hans van der Meij. 2004. Empirical proof for presenting screen captures in software documentation. *Technical Communication* 51 (2): 224-238.

GMAP (Government Management Accountability & Performance). *General guidelines*. Plain Talk, http://www.accountability.wa.gov/plaintalk/ptguidelines/default.asp (accessed December 15, 2007).

Gregory, Judy. 2004. Writing for the web versus writing for print: Are they really so different? *Technical Communication* 51 (2): 276-285.

Hayhoe, George F. 2000. What do technical communicators need to know? *Technical Communication* 47 (2): 151-153.

Helvetica. 2007. Gary Hustwit. London: Swiss Dots.

HHS (Health and Human Services Department). 2006. *Research-Based Web Design & Usability Guidelines*. Usability.gov, http://usability.gov/pdfs/guidelines.html (accessed September 25, 2007).

Hofmann, Patrick. 2004. The successes and challenges of visual language. *Intercom*, June, 16-18.

Horton, William. 1991. *Illustrating computer documentation: The art of presenting information graphically on paper and online*. New York: Wiley.

Isakson, Carol S., and Jan H. Spyridakis. 1999. The influence of semantics and syntax on what readers remember. *Technical Communication* 46 (3): 366-381.

Krull, Robert, Shreyas J. D'Souza, Debopriyo Roy, and D. Michael Sharp. 2004. Designing procedural illustrations. *IEEE Transactions on Professional Communication* 47 (1): 27-33.

Larson, Kevin. 2004. The science of word recognition or how I learned to stop worrying and love the bouma. Advanced Reading Technology, Microsoft Corporation, http://www.microsoft.com/typography/ctfonts/WordRecognition.aspx (accessed December 6, 2007).

Laskowski, Sharon J., and Janice (Ginny) Redish. 2006. Making ballot language understandable to voters. Presentation at USENIX/ACCURATE Electronic Voting Technology (EVT) Workshop, August 1, Vancouver, BC. http://www.usenix.org/events/evt06/tech/tech.html (accessed on December 7, 2007).

Locke, Joanne. 2004. A history of plain language in the United States government. PlainLanguage.gov, http://www.plainlanguage.gov/whatisPL/history/locke.cfm (accessed November 30, 2007).

Loorbach, Nicole, Joyce Karreman, and Michael Steehouder. 2007. Adding motivational elements to an instruction manual for seniors: Effects on usability and motivation. *Technical Communication* 54 (3): 343-358.

Mazur, Beth. 2000. Revisiting plain language. *Technical Communication* 47 (2): 205-211.

Meeker & Associates. Legibility. ClearviewHwy, http://clearviewhwy.com/ResearchAndDesign/legibilityStudies.php (accessed December 6, 2007).

Miller, George. 1956. The magical number seven, plus or minus two: Some limits on our capacity for processing information. http://www.musanim.com/miller1956 (accessed November 11, 2007). Originally published in *The Psychological Review*, 63 (1956): 81-97.

Mirel, Barbara, and Rachel Spilka. 2002. *Reshaping technical communication: New directions and challenges for the 21st century.* Mahwah, NJ: Lawrence Erlbaum Associates, Inc.

Morkes, John, and Jacob Nielsen. 1997. Concise, SCANNABLE, and objective: How to write for the Web. useit.com: Jakob Nielsen's Website, http://www.useit.com/papers/webwriting/writing.html (accessed November 30, 2007).

Morkes, John, and Jacob Nielsen. 1998. Applying writing guidelines to Web pages. useit.com: Jakob Nielsen's Website, http://www.useit.com/papers/webwriting/rewriting.html (accessed December 4, 2007).

Office of the Federal Register. 1998. Making regulations readable in *Document drafting handbook*, MMR-1-MMR-6. http://www.archives.gov/federal-register/write/plain-language/readable-regulations.pdf (accessed October 17, 2007).

PlainLanguage.gov. Federal plain language guidelines. http://www.plainlanguage.gov/howto/guidelines/reader-friendly.cfm (accessed October 15, 2007).

Poole, Alex. 2005. Which are more legible: Serif or sans serif typefaces? Alex Poole Interaction design and research, http://www.alexpoole.info/academic/literaturereview.html (accessed October 4, 2007).

Potsus, Whitney Beth. 2003. Adding life to your documentation. *Intercom*, November, 25-28.

Redish, Janice C. (Ginny). 1988. Reading to learn to do. *Technical Writing Teacher* 15 (3): 223-233. Reprinted in *IEEE Transactions on Professional Communication* 32 (1989) (4): 289-293.

Redish, Janice C. (Ginny). 1993. Understanding readers. In *Techniques for Technical Communicators*, ed. Carol Barnum and Saul Carliner, 14–41. New York: Macmillan.

Redish, Janice C. (Ginny). 1998. Minimalism in technical communication. In *Minimalism Beyond the Nurnberg Funnel*, ed. John M. Carroll, 219-245. Cambridge: The MIT Press.

Redish, Janice C. (Ginny). 2000. What is information design? *Technical Communication* 47 (2): 163-166.

Redish, Janice C. (Ginny). 2004a. Applying research to practice: What's relevant today? Presentation at the annual conference of the Society for Technical Communication, May 9-12, in Baltimore, MD. http://www.redish.net/content/handouts.html (accessed September 24, 2007).

Redish, Janice C. (Ginny). 2004b. Letting go of the words. *Intercom,* June, 5-10.

Redish, Janice C. (Ginny). 2006. Guidelines for writing clear instructions and messages for voters and poll workers. NIST (National Institute of Standards and Technology), http://vote.nist.gov/032906PlainLanguageRpt.pdf (accessed September 17, 2007).

Redish, Janice C. (Ginny). 2007. *Letting go of the words*. San Francisco: Morgan Kaufmann.

Redish, Janice C. (Ginny). Headings. PlainLanguage.gov, http://www.plainlanguage.gov/howto/guidelines/headings.cfm (accessed October 15, 2007).

Roebben, Nicolas, and Yves Bestgen. 2006. Reading and expertise: The impact of connectives on text comprehension in the financial field. In *Information and document design: Variety on the research*. Ed. Saul

Carliner, Jan Piet Verckens, and Cathy de Waele, 149-165. Amsterdam, The Netherlands: John Benjamins.

Roy, Debopriyo. 2006. Using graphic indicators to facilitate mechanical reasoning in procedural graphics. *Technical Communication* 53 (4): 447-463.

Salvo, Michael, Meredith W. Zoetewey, and Kate Agena. 2007. A case of exhaustive documentation: Re-centering system-oriented organizations around user need. *Technical Communication* 54 (1): 46-57.

Schriver, Karen. A. 1997. *Dynamics in document design.* New York: John Wiley & Sons.

Securities and Exchange Commission. 1998. *A plain English handbook: How to create clear SEC disclosure document.* http://www.sec.gov/pdf/handbook.pdf (accessed December 10, 2007).

Spyridakis, Jan H. 2000. Guidelines for authoring comprehensible web pages and evaluating their success. *Technical Communication* 47 (3): 359-382.

Spyridakis, Jan H., Laura D. Schultz, and Alexandra L. Bartell. 2005. Heading frequency and comprehension: Studies of print versus online media. In *Proceedings: STC's 52nd Annual Conference.* Society for Technical Communication. http://www.stc.org/ConfProceed/2005/PDFs/0032.pdf (accessed November 28, 2007).

Spyridakis, Jan H., and Michael J. Wenger. 1992. Writing for human performance: Relating reading research to document design. *Technical Communication* 39 (2): 202-215.

Steehouder, Michael. 2004. Acquiring procedural knowledge of a technology interface: introduction to this special issue. *IEEE Transactions on Professional Communication* 47 (1): 1 – 4.

Steehouder, Michael F., and Carel J. M. Jansen. 1996. The sequential order of instructions: Impact on text quality. In *Proceedings: STC's 43rd Annual Conference.* Society for Technical Communication. http://www.stc.org/confproceed/1996/PDFs/PG247250.PDF (accessed October 04, 2007).

Taylor, Conrad. 2000. Information design: A European perspective. *Technical Communication* 47 (2): 167-168.

van der Meij, Hans, and Mark Gellevij. 1998. Screen captures in software documentation. *Technical Communication* 45 (4): 529-543.

van der Waarde, Karel. 1999. Typographic dimensions and conventional wisdom: A discrepancy? *Technical Communication* 46 (1): 67-74.

Wright, Patricia. 1988. Issues of content and presentation in document design. In *Handbook of human-computer interaction*, ed. M. Helander, 629-652. New York: North-Holland.

Wright, Patricia. 1998. Printed instructions: Can research make a difference? In *Visual information for everyday use: Design and research perspectives*, ed. Harm J. G. Zwaga, Theo Boersema, and Henriette C. M. Hoonout, 45-66. London: Taylor and Francis.

Zimmerman, Donald E. and Terri Prickett. 2000. A usability case study: Prospective students' use of a university web page. In *Proceedings: STC's 47th Annual Conference*. Society for Technical Communication. http://www.stc.org/ConfProceed/2000/PDFs/00099.pdf (accessed December 4, 2007).

Appendix A: Prior Research and Resources

Prepared by

Dana E. Chisnell
Susan C. Becker

Review of relevant literature:
technical communication and information design

March, 2008

Contents

Review of relevant literature:
technical communication and information design

Deliverable: A summary review of the literature.

Background

The goal of this project on Voting System Documentation Usability and Poll Worker Usability Testing is to improve the usability of documentation used by poll workers and election support staff by developing these resources:

- Style guide incorporating best practices for voting system documentation

- Protocol for voting system test labs to use to measure the usability of instructions supplied by voting system manufacturers for election workers

The first step in developing the style guide of best practices is this review of relevant information from technical communication and information design literature. Here we review primary and secondary resources that form the thinking behind current best practices in technical communication as they apply to voting systems.

What is technical communication?

"Technical communication is the process of conveying usable information through writing or speech about a specific domain to an intended audience"[3].

When technical communication began to develop in support of the defense and aerospace industries in the decades after World War II, technical writers, like their audiences, were primarily technical experts. In the 1980s and 90s, consumer electronics outpaced these industries as the largest market for technical writing and ordinary people became the largest audience for information products. Since then "the ability to communicate clearly to nonexperts using a variety of media and information types has emerged as the hallmark of technical communication excellence" (Hayhoe 2000, 151).

The Society for Technical Communication (STC), the largest organization in the world dedicated to advancing the arts and sciences of technical communication, today defines technical communicators in part as those who:

> Develop and design instructional and informational tools needed to assure safe, appropriate and effective use of science and technology, intellectual property, and manufactured products and services (Burton 2007).

For our review, we focus on those aspects of technical communication most relevant to developing usable documentation of voting systems; that is, "information tools needed to assure safe, appropriate and effective use" of a manufactured product. We see these information tools primarily as procedures to support setting up voting systems, conducting polling, shutting down voting systems, and auditing voting systems. However, the tools also include descriptions, examples, illustrations, and other types of technical communication.

---

[3] Wikipedia contributors, "Technical communication," *Wikipedia, The Free Encyclopedia*, http://en.wikipedia.org/w/index.php?title=Technical_communication&oldid=175489633 (accessed December 15, 2007).

What we looked for

We looked for sources that discussed the current thinking in best practices in technical communication and information design. We considered primary and secondary sources from technical communication and information design, as well as instructional design, linguistics, reading, cognitive psychology, and human-computer interaction.

Although we focused on sources that used research-based approaches, we also considered those that discuss conventions as well as current trends.

Where we looked

We began by drawing on our experience as practitioners working in technical communication, information architecture, usability testing, instructional design, and teaching, as well as our experience working with NIST and Ginny Redish on the language in instructions on ballots, to create a list of the main research topics in these areas that are especially relevant to writing documentation for voting systems.

We expanded and refined this list by studying other literature reviews and guidelines. In particular, two extensive literature reviews support many of the ideas we cover in this review.

The first, *Document Design: A Review of the Relevant Research* (Felker and others 1980), was developed as part of the Document Design Project, which was funded by the Department of Education. This review and the *Guidelines for Document Designers* (Felker and others 1981) that resulted have provided the basis and set the agenda for much of the discussion in technical communication and document design since the 80s. We used the summaries of early research from these documents in our review.

The second, *Research-Based Web Design & Usability Guidelines* (HHS 2006), developed by the U.S. Department of Health and Human Services (HHS), though not primarily a literature review, includes the over 450 research sources to support its extensive list of guidelines. Although most documentation provided by voting system manufacturers is delivered in print or is meant to be printed, we reviewed the *Research-Based Web Design & Usability Guidelines* as well as other research and guidelines for writing for online presentation and the Web because we believe that they are often relevant to writing for print documentation. (See our discussion of the similarities between writing for print and writing for the web on page 93.) Also, though this review focuses on writing for print, we believe more of the documentation of voting systems will eventually move from print to online presentation.

We reviewed several guidelines from the Plain Language movement, including the *Federal Plain Language Guidelines* (PlainLanguage.gov), *Federal Register Document Drafting Handbook* (Office of the Federal Register 1998), *Washington's Plain Talk Guidelines* (GMAP), and, of course, the *Guidelines for Writing Clear Instructions and Messages for Voters and Poll Workers* (Redish 2006).

We also reviewed several recent works on major directions in research on technical communication written by academics and other researchers in the field; for example, "Current challenges of research in information and document design" (Carliner 2006), "The State of Research in Technical Communication" (Blakeslee and Spilka 2004), and *Reshaping Technical Communication: New Directions and Challenges for the 21st Century* (Mirel and Spilka 2002). These documents helped us determine the role research has played in technical communication and how it may influence future directions.

All of these sources helped us determine the basic theories of technical communication that people working or doing research in the field generally agree upon today. From these sources, we followed up many of the references we found in those studies, articles, and books that support the theories. We supplemented our sources by searching on the Internet (Google, Google Scholar) and in online libraries and newsletters (ACM Digital Library, Ingenta, Human Factors International, EServer Technical Communication Library).

How we dealt with the quantity of available resources

The challenge we faced in writing a review of the literature and research that pertains to technical communication and information design in the 21st century is the quantity of research generated over the past sixty years, and especially since 1980.

For example, Alred's 2003 "Essential Works on Technical Communication" presents an annotated list of 115 essential works compiled from a list of over 600 titles. One of those, *The St. Martin's bibliography of business and technical communication* includes 376 works (Alred 2003).

The authors of the 2006 *Research-Based Web Design & Usability Guidelines* at usability.gov reduced their initial 500 guidelines to the current 187, but those are based on over 450 listed resources. A panel of 18 experts assigned "Strength of Evidence" ratings for the guidelines.

Within the scope of this review, we could not read all the sources that we wanted to use. Though we do include several primary sources, we have also relied on secondary sources and on their summaries of other primary and secondary sources.

What we found

As might be expected, although some early directions in technical communication have become less important as technology has evolved, most have continued to be developed and refined by more recent research. And of course new ideas are developing.

In this review, we focus on the issues that we believe are the most helpful in improving and assuring the usability of the documentation of voting systems. We cover major concepts that have been generally accepted since the 1980s (for example, the use of common words rather than jargon) as well as major issues that have been developing since then (such as skimming and scanning behavior in reading), and especially in more recent years (for example, the use of screenshots in software documentation).

The review focuses on the following issues:

How Information and document design continue to evolve

- Plain language movement made government documents clearer

- Technological advances broaden the definition of document design

- Information design and document design are merging

- Plain language, usability are gaining momentum

- Writing for print and writing for the web are similar

What we know about readers and users

- People use manuals to find the information they need to do their work

- Readers skim and scan information rather than reading carefully

- Readers interpret as they read and act on the first reasonable option

- Setting the context helps users understand and complete instructions

- People can process only a limited amount of information at a time

- Readers comprehend more when the topic is interesting or familiar

What we know about information design

- Documents that are user-oriented are easier to comprehend

- Headings and other "signals" help readers comprehend text

- Information presented in a logical order is easier to understand

- Information presented first is easier to remember

What we know about words, sentences and paragraphs

- Common words and short words are easier to understand
- Short, simple sentences are easier to comprehend and remember

What we know about graphics and illustrations

- Graphics are understood more quickly than words
- Graphics and text together are more effective than words
- Graphics help users decide when to switch from instructions to a task
- Screenshots help users comprehend documentation

What we know about typography

- Mixed-case is easier to read than all upper case
- Emphasizing text helps but too much emphasis can be distracting
- Serif and sans serif are equally legible
- Leading and line length affect legibility
- Ragged right alignment is preferred by document designers
- Typefaces have emotional content

Information and document design continue to evolve

- Plain language movement made government documents clearer
- Technological advances broaden the definition of document design
- Information design and document design are merging
- Plain language, usability are gaining momentum
- Writing for print and writing for the web are similar

Plain language movement made government documents clearer

In the 1960s and especially the 1970s, the plain language movement in the United States, supported by Presidents Nixon and Carter, worked to make government documents easier for the citizens who used them to understand (Carliner 2006; Locke 2004; Schriver 1997). Other countries have also been involved in the plain language movements for even longer than the US (Locke 2004; Mazur 2000; Schriver 1997).

One result was the Document Design Project, which studied the problems of public documents and helped agencies implement plain language. It created *Document Design: A Review of the Relevant Research* and the *Guidelines for Document Designers*, which served as a handbook for government writers for many years (Locke 2004).

However, President Reagan rescinded President Carter's Executive Orders, and within the Federal Government, the plain language movement made limited progress during the 1980s (Locke 2004).

Although the research community supported government action to improve writing, there was some discussion about its definition of the audience and its methods for evaluating documents.[4] By the mid-1980s, the research community replaced studies in plain language with "more broadly conceived efforts in document design [which] examined readers' actual comprehension and use of documents" as well as their responses to visual language (Schriver 1997, 29).

Technological advances broaden the definition of document design

The technological advances of the 1980s, which included the first practical personal computers and desktop publishing, also changed the way documents were produced and the nature of documents themselves (Schriver 1997). Researchers (and technical writers) worked to understand the most effective ways to communicate with the new

---

[4] Mazur (2000) refutes these criticisms of plain language in a discussion of its past and current resources.

technology, while also beginning to look at ways to make documents more usable (Carliner 2006).

As web technology exploded in the 1990s, technical communicators were joined by other information providers in developing ways to organize and present information online. In particular, those with a background in library science developed the concepts of information architecture, which is concerned with organizing and labeling websites and other online environments to support usability.

Information design and document design are merging

For technical communication, two concepts continue to be central: document design and information design. Some technical communicators make a distinction between these, defining document design as the way information is presented (layout, typography, color, and so on) and information design as the "overall process of developing a successful document" (Redish 2000, 163).

For example, Carliner (2006) distinguishes between the two:

> Document design focuses on providing readers with physical markers that help them find content of interest and with the general appearance of information so it is both pleasing and usable (2).

> Information design takes a broader perspective, focusing on the meaning-making of text…specifically…preparing communication products so that they achieve the performance objectives established for them (2-3).

Schriver (1997) defines document design as "a field concerned with creating texts (broadly defined) that integrate words and pictures in ways that help people to achieve their specific goals for using texts at home, school, or work (10)."

Others, including Redish (2000), use information design to describe both the overall process and the presentation of information on the page or screen. And Carliner (2006) concedes that the two terms are merging as indicated by the merging of the *Information Design Journal* and *Document Design* into a single journal.[5]

For our purposes, we generally use the terms interchangeably and note that technical communication is now concerned with both information

---

[5] The European tradition of information design involves a broader scope, "to improve the design of information artifacts and systems encountered by people in every part of their daily lives," such as wayfinding in museums and other public places, not just documentation (Taylor 2000, 167).

design and document design, and how they relate to each other (Redish 2000).

Plain language, usability are gaining momentum

In 1998, President Clinton, in a memorandum that requires all new federal regulations to be written in plain language, stated:

> Plain language documents have logical organization; common, everyday words, except for necessary technical terms; 'you' and other pronouns; the active voice; and short sentences (Locke 2004).

Clinton's description reaffirms many of the basic ideas of plain language as well as good information design.

In 1998, the Securities and Exchange Commission published *A Plain English Handbook: How to create clear SEC disclosure documents*, which "remains an excellent resource on plain language writing" (Locke 2004).[6]

In 2001, the Washington State Department of Labor and Industries started "Plain Talk," a project to rewrite their form letters in Plain English (Botka 2002). The project was so successful that in 2005, Governor Christine O. Gregoire issued an executive order that all agencies adopt the principles and practices of Plain Talk.

In the current decade, several other movements in technical communication have gained momentum: the role of usability research in document design, the Internet as a means of delivering content, and research-based heuristics, such as the *Research-Based Web Design & Usability Guidelines* at www.usability.gov (Carliner 2006).

Writing for print and writing for the web are similar

Many of the discussions of writing for the web in the workplace started with the premise that writing for the web was different from writing for print, that it needed to be clearer, more concise, more aware of chunking, organized more clearly with precise headings, links and navigation.

But Gregory (2004) presents arguments to show that many of the underlying principles of writing apply to both print and online and have a long history in writing for print. For example, the suggestion that web authors should provide 50% less content is similar to the basic guidelines for Plain Language to have fewer words and shorter sentences. The idea

---

[6] Many US federal agencies have plain-language programs, including the Federal Aviation Administration, the Federal Register, the Food and Drug Administration, Health and Human Services, National Institutes of Health, and Veteran's Benefits Administration (Locke 2004).

that readers skim, which is the basis for writing scannable text, applies to both online and print, as does the idea that readers go directly to the information they need rather than reading cover-to-cover or from the top. The importance of "chunking" information, which is a common guideline for web writing, has been discussed as dividing information into coherent sections at least since the Document Design Project in 1980.

Similarly, Spyridakis (2000) found in her review that researchers in the 1980s believed that print documents and hypertext were significantly different in that print documents were linear, but hypertext documents were not. But more recent research showed that the two media are similar, that readers move around in both and then read when they locate the information they want.

Spyridakis (2000) also found that research in the 1980s and 90s, on how the medium (paper versus online) affects reading comprehension and recall, were not conclusive: some found better performance with print, some with online, and some with neither.

Of course, there is a danger in using research based on a context, on a specific communications challenge, to create more universal heuristic guidelines. Some researchers question whether results of research can be generalized from one population to another, from print-based to online or online to print, or from a single publication to any document (Carliner 2006). Carliner (2006) points out that we have "a need for more specific guidelines on communication than the research currently provides" (13). However, despite its shortcomings, research and theory based on research can provide a corrective (or at least augment) for what Brumberger (2004) calls, in speaking of typography, "the practitioners' lore and intuition" (13).

What we know about readers and users

- People use manuals to find the information they need to do their work

- Readers skim and scan information rather than reading carefully

- Readers interpret as they read and act on the first reasonable option

- Setting the context helps users understand and complete instructions

- People can process only a limited amount of information at a time

- Readers comprehend more when the topic is interesting or familiar

People use manuals to find the information they need to do their work

"In daily life, people do not follow all the instructions that they encounter, only those relating to the goals that they currently have" (Wright 1998, 52).

Users of software and hardware are focused on their own task and are seldom in a learning or study mode. They turn to manuals to find what they need in order to accomplish their immediate goal and then get back to it. They are usually "reading to do" when they turn to manuals, rather than reading to learn or even reading to learn to do (Redish 1998, 1993, 1988).

Users turn to manuals when:

- They don't know what tasks they need to complete to reach a goal.

- They don't know the steps for a specific task.

- They have a problem, whether they can state it clearly or not (Redish 1998).

Schriver (1997) found that, of the users that she surveyed, only 23% reported that they read the instructions before they tried a new function, 42% said they read the instructions while they tried the new function, 17% said they referred to the instructions only when they were confused, and 19% said they did not use the instructions at all.

Readers seldom go to manuals for conceptual information (Redish 1998).

Wright says that the questions people ask of technical information are problem-driven ("Why didn't that work?") or task-driven ("How do I do that?"). They are not usually system-driven ("How does it work?") (Redish 1998, 20).[7]

---

[7] Redish is referring to Patricia Wright (1988).

Readers skim and scan information rather than reading carefully

The idea that readers scan has appeared in discussions of technical writing frequently since 1981 (Gregory 2004). Readers of both print and online documents scan information rather than reading it thoroughly (Redish 2004b).

Schriver (1997) found that roughly 80% of the consumers she surveyed reported that they scanned their instruction manuals or used them as a reference—46% of the users said they scanned them; 35% said they used the documents for reference (they went to a specific page to get a specific piece of information).

Studies of how people read on the Web found that they also scan and that sites that are more scannable are easier to use. A study of five different writing styles found that a sample Web site scored 47% higher in measured usability when it was designed to be scannable; that is, it had bulleted lists, boldface text to highlight key words, photo captions, shorter sections of text, and more headings than the control site. Users performed tasks faster, made fewer errors, and recalled the content of the site better (Morkes and Nielsen 1997).

Readers interpret as they read and act on the first reasonable option

Research shows that people tend to act as soon as they see something that talks about action. They do not wait to finish the sentence if the context for that action is at the end of the sentence. They do not read to the end of a paragraph even if a caution about the action comes later in the paragraph (Carroll 1990; Redish 1988, 1993).

Carroll (1990) observed that users tended to act before reading instructions. He describes the paradox of sense making that users of a new program face: To interact meaningfully with a new program, users need to acquire certain skills and understanding. But they can acquire these only through meaningful interaction with the program. Faced with this paradox, users tend to pick the first reasonable action rather than learn all possible actions and pick the best.

People reading voting machine documentation also act in this way, especially poll workers on Election Day who are under pressure to keep the voters moving through the polling place.

Setting the context helps users understand and complete instructions

On the sentence level, readers also act as soon as they see a reasonable option, even if their initial interpretation might be incorrect. Research shows that when the general organizational information comes first, readers understand directions more easily and they make fewer mistakes (Dixon 1987). That is, when the context is set before the action, readers can follow directions more successfully.

Dixon (1987) investigated what people did with instructions that had two parts, general organizational information (context) and component step information (actions), depending on the order of the parts.

This is an example from the study, with the context first:

> This will be a picture of a wine glass.
> Draw a triangle on top of an upside-down T.

This is an example with the action first:

> Draw a triangle on top of an upside-down T.
> This will be a picture of a wine glass.

Dixon was especially interested in what the readers would do when the action came first: would they hold the information in memory until they had the context, or would they guess the context and act immediately. The results showed that they guessed and did not wait. When the context came first, most readers drew a wine glass; when the action came first, many drew a Christmas tree.[8]

Dixon theorized that users sometimes make errors in following directions because they misinterpret how the steps are organized and work together. He suggested that "the problem could be alleviated by providing initially some high-level information about the nature and organization of the task" (Dixon 1987, 33). That is, some context.

Brief overviews, such as lists of headings, graphics, flowcharts, or short sets of questions and answers, help users understand instructions (Redish 1998). Redish and Dumas also showed that providing this type of information, even in a manual that users turn to only when they need to find information to complete a task, helps them learn (Redish 1998).

Poll workers who are setting up voting machines under stressful conditions (early hours, an unfamiliar setting, time pressure, a machine they may have never seen before) may easily misinterpret directions, especially if they simply follow step-by-step instructions that do not provided them with a context.

---

[8] Thanks to Sharon J. Laskowski and Ginny Redish, for this framing of Dixon's work in their presentation *Making Ballot Language Understandable to Voters* (Laskowski and Redish 2006).

People can process only a limited amount of information at a time

Miller (1956) first showed that short-term or working memory is limited in the number of elements it can contain simultaneously. According to a model Ganier (2004) discusses, "cognitive processes involved in the processing of instructions occur in working memory, which is constrained in both time and processing capacity" (16).

When readers need to remember more information than they can handle in their working memory while performing a procedure, they experience a "cognitive load" which can lead to errors (Steehouder and Jansen 1996).

Cognitive psychology has shown that people use a strategy of grouping or organizing information into chunks to increase the amount of information they can hold in short-term memory (Miller 1956).[9]

Chunking, which is discussed extensively in guidelines for writing for online presentation, is also an important technique in writing documentation for print (Redish 1993; Gregory 2004). In technical writing and information design literature, "chunking" refers to breaking text into short pieces, often with meaningful headings. Research that Spyridakis and Wenger (1992) reviewed showed that chunking decreases the demands on the reader's memory and improves comprehension.

Many procedure writers also follow the short-term memory rule-of-thumb that the length of a list should be no more than seven, plus or minus two, based on Miller (1956) *Psychology Review* article. But analysis of Miller's article since then has shown that seven is not the "magical number" he thought it to be (Doumont 2002). Bailey (2000) reports that various researchers have suggested the working memory capacity is actually four to six items, four items, or three items.

But considering that people read to do and once they have found an actionable instruction move to perform it, the limits of working memory do not need to limit the length of a list of procedures. There is no expectation that the audience needs to memorize the list even for a short time.

---

[9] "In cognitive psychology and mnemonics, chunking refers to a strategy for making more efficient use of short-term memory by recoding information. More generally, Herbert Simon has used the term chunk to indicate long-term memory structures that can be used as units of perception and meaning, and chunking as the learning mechanisms leading to the acquisition of these chunks." Wikipedia contributors. Chunking (psychology). *Wikipedia, The Free Encyclopedia.*
http://en.wikipedia.org/wiki/Chunking_%28psychology%29 (accessed December 4, 2007).

Readers comprehend more when the topic is interesting or familiar

Research shows that "readers comprehend better and retain more information when they are interested in the topic of the passage" (Isakson and Spyridakis 1999, 367).

Isakson and Spyridakis (1999) found in their research that "readers recall information they perceive to be more important more frequently than information they perceive to be less important" (377). A recent study on motivational elements in instruction manuals for seniors found that adding motivational elements improved task performance (Loorbach, Joyce, and Steehouder 2007).

Research also shows that prior knowledge can assist comprehension, although one study showed prior knowledge had no effect (Isakson and Spyridakis 1999).

Cognitive psychology teaches us that "users construct their own mental models (schemas), combining new information from what they see in interfaces and documentation with what they already have in their minds from earlier experiences" (Redish 1998, 220). Prior knowledge can help users understand and incorporate new information more quickly. But it can also result in their jumping to conclusions about the new information, trying to match it to their existing mental models which may not be appropriate (Carroll 1990).

What we know about information design

- Documents that are user-oriented are easier to comprehend
- Headings and other "signals" help readers comprehend text
- Information presented in a logical order is easier to understand
- Information presented first is easier to remember

Documents that are user-oriented are easier to comprehend

Carroll (1990) in his work on minimalism in instructional design found that instructional manuals based on users' tasks were more effective than those based on a comprehensive presentation of system-related tasks. Carroll argues that you cannot design training "that is both usable and comprehensive" (93). The goal of minimalism is "to teach people what they need to learn in order to do what they wish to do" (Carroll 1990, 3) rather than trying to teach them a conceptual model of how the system works.

Redish (1998) reaffirmed the importance of focusing on the user in her argument for a user-centered process for documentation: "Extensive, iterative interactions with users and making sure of what is learned in those interactions is critical to successful documentation" (236).

Salvo, Zoetewey, and Agena (2007) showed that product documentation that is system oriented and written without consideration of how it would be used or under what circumstances "can be overwhelming for target-audience end users" as well as expensive for manufacturers (48).

Schriver (1997) demonstrated that it is critical to consider the readers' thoughts and feelings when designing documents that inform or persuade. When the document designers did not take the real readers seriously, the documents were ineffective even when the readers could comprehend them. In addition, the image of the organization behind the documents suffered. "Failing to consider the knowledge and values of the real audience can create a lasting negative identity for the organization that may take years to shake" (204).

With voter confidence already low, documentation of voting systems needs to be user-centered not only to help poll workers use the machines to accomplish their tasks, but also to convey an image of the voting system manufacturers as people who are concerned about making voting run smoothly on Election Day and providing fair results. User-centered documents can do both more effectively than system-centered documentation.

Headings and other "signals" help readers comprehend text

Research shows that when readers encounter "signals" in print text, they are able to better comprehend new or difficult information. "These signals—headings, summaries, overview sentences, and other types of cues about text content—help readers create…a structural and content-based context that helps readers take in new information" (Spyridakis, Schultz, and Bartell 2005, 138).

Headings help users determine where they are in a document and a task. They help users orient themselves and make the right associations with their pre-existing concepts or schemas (Redish 2004a). Research shows that headings also "provide clues about information importance" (Spyridakis, Schultz, and Bartell 2005, 138) and they help people find information faster (Redish on PlainLanguage.gov). Perhaps for that reason, they are important in making text scannable in online documents (Morkes and Nielsen 1997).

People also prefer that documents have headings. They believe that documents with headings are easier to read and understand, and they are more motivated to use them (Redish on PlainLanguage.gov).

To be effective, headings need to focus on the users' tasks, not the system (Redish 1998). Headings need to "make connections to the user." Nouns and noun phrases are not as effective as questions and phrases that include verbs and people, for example, personal pronouns (Redish on PlainLanguage.gov).

Good headings help users form a goal and monitor their progress toward it. Users are able to process instructions more efficiently if they are given precise headings that correspond to their goals (Ganier 2004). For example, if the poll worker's goal is to override an error and accept a voter's ballot as is, a heading might be "Accepting a voter's ballot when there is an error message" or "Overriding an error message when a voter requests it."

Causal connectives (for example, *because*) are another type of signal. Roebben and Bestgen (2006) showed that when causal connectives were included in texts "low expertise level readers as well as high expertise level readers learned more from coherent texts (with connectives) than less coherent text (without connectives)" (149).

Information presented in a logical order is easier to understand

Information that is presented in a logical order is easier for the readers to understand. This is especially true for series of steps in a procedure. In particular, time-based sequences are easily understood by users.

Research shows that "the sequence of verbal information can determine how information is stored in memory and retrieved" and that randomly or arbitrarily reordering sentences decreased learning (Felker and others 1980, 56).

Steehouder and Jansen (2004) argue that "the sequential order of procedural steps is crucial for effective and efficient performance." They describe three "rules" for optimizing instructions:

- First things first: put instructions in an order that prevents users from neglecting important steps.

- Minimize cognitive load: put instructions in an order that allows readers to forget what they read.

- Save time and effort: put instructions in an order that "on average" requires as little time as possible of the readers. (247)

Information presented first is easier to remember

Research shows that readers recall information better when it is presented first (primacy) or last (recency) in lists rather than in the middle of lists. One study of prose found that recall of propositions in text was highest from first to last to middle in two of eight passages. Another prose study found only primacy effects. Yet another study found both primacy and recency effects (Isakson and Spyridakis 1999).

These studies indicate that information presented last is also easier to remember. However, as we discussed, readers interpret as they read and respond to the first reasonable option. So we believe that, under normal circumstances, the recall of the last item is not relevant.

Dixon (1987) also notes that procedural directions are read faster when general organizational information is found at the beginning rather than at the end of directions.

What we know about words, sentences and paragraphs

- Common words and short words are easier to understand
- Short, simple sentences are easier to comprehend and remember

Common words and short words are easier to understand

The seminal texts on Document Design, *Document Design: A Review of Relevant Research* (Felker and others 1980) and *Guidelines for Document Designers* (Felker and others 1981), cite studies and reviews of studies that support these ideas:

- Less frequent and harder words take longer to recognize.
- Harder words are harder to remember.
- Sentences and text containing harder words take longer to read and reading takes more effort.
- Sentences with harder words take longer to use.
- Concrete words are easier to learn and recall than abstract words.

Spyridakis has discussed additional research before and since 1980 that shows that high-frequency words (words that are used frequently in the English language) and short words are easier for readers to recognize and comprehend than their low-frequency or longer counterparts (Spyridakis 2000; Isakson and Spyridakis 1999; Spyridakis and Wenger 1992).

Spyridakis also notes additional research showing that "words that represent concrete concepts are encoded more quickly and accurately, recalled more often, and comprehended better than words that represent abstract concepts" (Spyridakis 2000, 368).

A more recent study found that perspective students in a usability test of university websites had difficulty using the sites because they did not understand the universities' terminology and jargon (Zimmerman and Prickett 2000).

Common words and short words may be easier to read because of the way we recognize words. Evidence from the last 20 years of work in cognitive psychology indicates that readers use the letters within a word to recognize a word. "We recognize a word's component letters, then use that visual information to recognize a word. In addition to perceptual information, we also use contextual information to help recognize words during ordinary reading" (Larson 2004).

Short, simple sentences are easier to comprehend and remember

Felker and others (1981), in *Guidelines for Document Designers*, cited studies that show that short sentences are easier to read and understand. They also noted other factors that can affect comprehension, including whether a sentence is concrete or abstract, grammatically complex, or sparse or dense with information. They concluded that, although the length of the sentence is important, "it is not sufficient in itself to ensure that the sentence will be easy to understand" (43).

Syntax (the way words are grammatically formed and ordered to form phrases, clauses, and sentences) can affect comprehension and recall.

Research in the 1970s and 80s showed that readers recall independent clauses faster than clauses that cannot stand alone as a sentence (dependent clauses). Readers also showed poorer comprehension of important information in dependent clauses than of important information in independent clauses (Isakson and Spyridakis 1999).

Embedded clauses (clauses inside other clauses, often seen after relative pronouns like who, that, or which) can also cause problems (Redish 2004a). Research shows that readers make more comprehension errors with relative clauses that are embedded in the middle of a sentence than they do with those at the end of a sentence (Isakson and Spyridakis 1999; Spyridakis and Wenger 1992).

Isakson and Spyridakis (1999) found that readers were more likely to recall information when it was in clauses (rather than phrases or other structures) or independent clauses (rather than dependent clauses, relative clauses, or other structures). Readers also recalled information in relative clauses that were at the end of the sentence better than in relative clauses embedded in the middle of the sentence. But the researchers were not sure whether that was because of the location of the relative clause or of the information itself at the end of the sentence.

Two studies of Web sites by Morkes and Nielsen (1997, 1998) showed that Web sites with concisely written text were more usable. The 1997 study of different writing styles found that a sample Web site scored 58% higher in measured usability when it was written concisely; that is, written with much shorter text. The combined version, which was written concisely, written for scannability, and stripped of "marketese," scored 124% higher in measured usability.

In the 1998 study, Morkes and Nielsen redesigned a Web site following writing guidelines to make the site "concise, easy to scan, and objective (rather than promotional) in style." They report that "the rewritten website scored 159% higher than the original in measured usability."

What we know about graphics and illustrations

- Graphics are understood more quickly than words

- Graphics and text together are more effective than words

- Graphics help users decide when to switch from instructions to a task

- Screenshots help users comprehend documentation

Graphics are understood more quickly than words

According to models of picture and text comprehension, we process pictures and text differently. Building a mental model from text requires more resources and so creates a heavier cognitive load than building a mental model from pictures (Ganier 2004).[10]

When people use instructions to operate a new piece of equipment, adding pictures can "reduce the cognitive load and enhance the elaboration of a mental model" because of the similarity of the picture and the equipment and perhaps the user's internal representations (Ganier 2004, 21).

Pictures are often easier to remember than verbal descriptions (Horton 1991; Felker and others 1980, 35).

Graphics and text together are more effective than words

Research prior to 1980 showed that graphics, including pictures, drawings, graphs, flowcharts, and tables, are often better than text at making certain kinds of relationships clear. One study found that the most appropriate presentation depends on the nature and difficulty of the problem. For example, "tables are the quickest for solving easy problems, if the user knows what to look for," but "flowcharts are the most accurate, especially if the user does not know what to look for, or if the problem is hard." The study also found that "bureaucratic prose…yields the slowest and least-accurate problem solving" (Felker and others 1981, 35).

Since the 1980s, more studies have shown that using a mixed format of text and pictures leads to better performance than just text or pictures alone (Ganier 2004; Gellevij and van der Meij 2004).

Boekelder and Steehouder (1998) tested the effects of instructions that were presented in prose steps, a decision table, a flowchart, a logical

---

[10] "According to [current models of text and picture comprehension], text would lead to the construction of internal verbal representations and then to propositional representations that would allow the user to build a situational or a mental model. In contrast, a picture is considered as an external model (an analogical visual representation) that allows a more direct construction of a mental model." (Ganier 2004, 21)

tree, or a yes/no tree. The study showed that performance was best with a flowchart, logical tree, or yes/no tree, and worst with prose steps or decision table. The study also showed that the participants generally preferred the format they were used to (the one they used during the study), even when it was not the most effective, with the exception of the prose format. They preferred any graphical format to prose.

Interestingly, Boekelder and Steehouder (1998) did not include a continuous prose version because of the "unanimous results of the experiments reported in the literature. Graphical formats proved to be more effective and efficient than prose in all experiments" (234).

Hoffman (2004) describes a project in which he and his colleagues developed a "wordless" installation manual for a network computer. The manual, which was produced for a global audience, provided instructions with illustrations only. Navigation within a document (the table of contents) and between documents was also provided by illustrations. Usability testing and customer surveys indicated that the documentation was successful, especially in the eastern Asian market.

Graphics help users decide when to switch from instructions to a task

When users of hardware and software turn to a manual for information to complete a task, they do not read an entire procedure and then act on it, but instead switch from the text to the equipment and then back, if they need more information. The user decides when to switch one way or the other, though generally, the best time to switch is right after reading a single step (Boekelder and Steehouder 1998). From this we also conclude that writing steps that contain just one action could facilitate switching at the best time.

Boekelder and Steehouder (1999) showed that when sentences were ruled or boxed off (that is, when a line appeared across the page after each sentence) readers switched from reading to action at that point more often than when the lines were not there. Readers did this even when it was not the best time to do so; for example, when more than one action was included in a box, readers postponed the action until they read the whole box.

Screenshots help users comprehend documentation

Gellevij and van der Meij (2004) showed that users benefit from screen captures (screenshots) in software documentation. Screen captures when combined with text help the user:

- Develop a mental model of the way the program works and how it is structured

- Identify and locate window elements and objects

- Verify screen states and so recover from errors

Gellevij and van der Meij (2004) also believed that screenshots can help users determine when to switch between the documentation and the screen. But the study showed that users switched appropriately whether the documentation included screen captures or not. Gellevij and van der Meij suggest that their users already had a good basic "switching mode."[11]

---

[11] In a previous article, van der Meij and Gellevij (1998) provide an in-depth review of the literature and discuss the functions of screen captures that their 2004 study confirms.

What we know about typography

- Mixed-case is easier to read than all upper case
- Emphasizing text helps but too much emphasis can be distracting
- Serif and sans serif are equally legible
- Leading and line length affect legibility
- Ragged right alignment is preferred by document designers
- Typefaces have emotional content

Mixed-case is easier to read than all upper case

Research shows that reading speed is optimal when uppercase and lower case letters are used. Reading speed is slower when text is all capital letters (Schriver 1997; Felker and others 1981).[12]

Although its relationship with printed documentation may be tenuous, Clearview-Condensed, a font developed for road signs provides some additional arguments against using all capital letters. The developers of the font found that when the upper/lowercase Clearview-Condensed was compared to the most commonly used all-capital-letter typeface, "there was a 14 percent increase in recognition when viewed by older drivers at night, with no loss of legibility. When the size of Clearview-Condensed was increased by 12 percent to equal the overall footprint of the uppercase display, the recognition gain doubled to 29 percent with little change in overall sign size" (Meeker & Associates; Garvery, Pietrucha, and Meeker 1997).

Emphasizing text helps but too much emphasis can be distracting

Research reviewed by Felker and others (1981) shows that emphasizing specific information in text, using typographic clues, such as bolding, italics, font style, font size, and case, can help readers understand and remember the information. The research shows that readers understand and remember highlighted information better. However, combining techniques or overusing them can be confusing for the reader. The research also shows that **bold** is a better way to show emphasis than UPPERCASE.

Serif and sans serif are equally legible

Reviews of the research literature by Poole (2005), Bailey (2002a), and Schriver (1997) show that serif and sans serif fonts are equally legible A

---

[12] Reading lower case text faster is the result of practice; most readers spend most of their time reading lower case text and so are better at it (Larson 2004). However, we believe that this will most likely continue to be the case.

study by Arditi and Cho (2005) found "no difference in legibility between typefaces that differ only in the presence or absence of serifs" (1).

Though an earlier study reviewed by Schriver (1997) found serif and sans serif fonts equally preferred, Bailey (2002a) concluded from his review, that "most users tend to prefer sans serif fonts."

When testing online fonts, Bernard, Liao, and Mills (2001) found an effect for type size when they compared reading efficiency between serif and sans serif type fonts with 27 adults between the ages of 62 and 83. Overall, participants read 14-point type faster than 12-point type. When given a choice, participants also preferred 14-point type over 12-point type. However, Bernard and his team found that participants read the 14-point serif type fastest. (One untested theory is that the participants in Bernard's study may have read serif type faces fastest because they are accustomed to reading newsprint, whereas younger adults may be more accustomed to reading text in other media which tend to use sans serif typefaces.)

Leading and line length affect legibility

Research on how line length affects reading speed has been going on since 1881—over 125 years! Early research in 1881, 1883, and 1929, set the optimal length between 3 and 4 inches (Bailey 2002b).

For about the last fifty years, research and typographic guidelines have suggested an optimum line length of 10 to 12 words per line, or about 50 to 70 characters, for most conventional type sizes (9 to 12 points) (Felker and others 1981; Shriver 1997).

Typography experts hesitate to make guidelines about line length and when they do they tend to disagree (Shriver 1997). And actual practice does not always reflect the suggested guidelines (van der Waarde 1999). But in general, designers of instruction guides lean toward the lower end of the recommendation (8 or 9 words a line).

Leading refers to the space between lines. Leading interacts with type size and line length, so for example, large type usually requires more leading. Research reviewed by Shriver (1997) shows that readers dislike type that has either no space between lines (is "set solid") or too much leading (4 points of leading with 10-point type) and people read faster when the text is set to 1 to 4 points of leading than when text is set solid.

Guidelines usually reflect these findings, but as with line length, they are not always followed in general practice (van der Waarde 1999).

Research on the affects of line length on reading speed and comprehension on the web shows that

> Longer line lengths typically result in faster reading times, but research suggests medium to short line lengths typically may result in higher comprehension. In terms of columnar text, the research supports both long single columns of text, and multiple short columns while preference seems to lie towards multiple short columns (Baker 2005).

Ragged right alignment is preferred by document designers

Ragged right (flush left) text is aligned on the left margin with a ragged right margin like this report. Justified text is aligned along the left margin, and letter- and word-spacing is adjusted so that the text is also flush with the right margin.

Research reviewed by Felker and all (1981) and Schriver (1997) shows little difference in reading comprehension between ragged right text and justified text, except possibly for slow readers.

However, justified text can have unequal spaces between words that can create "rivers" or paths of blank space running vertically through the text. Rivers can affect reading speed negatively (Schriver 1997). But generally ragged right alignment is used because it is preferred by document designers.

Baker (2005) examined how multiple columns and text justification affect online reading of a narrative passage in terms of reading speed, comprehension, and satisfaction. He found that fast readers did best with two-column full-justified text and slow readers did best with a single column of non-justified text.

This research of text alignment of both print and online documents suggests that ragged-right is the most appropriate for poll workers. Whether poll workers are fast or slow readers, we believe they would function more like slow readers, in the environment of Election Day at the polls.

Typefaces have emotional content

Brumberger (2004, 2003a, 2003b), through extensive work on the rhetoric of typography, found that readers perceive typefaces and text to have personality attributes. Readers can also determine if typefaces are appropriate or inappropriate for a particular text (for example, a "direct" font like Arial is appropriately used for a professional text or inappropriately used for a "friendly text").

However, in Brumberger's study the persona of the typeface did not have a significant impact on reading comprehension or reading time. Also, the font did not change the reader's perception of the text; that is, a "friendly" font did not make the readers think the document was "friendly."

For a less theoretical treatment of the emotional content and impact of typefaces, see *Helvetica*, the feature-length independent film about typography, graphic design and global visual culture. "It looks at the proliferation of one typeface (which is celebrating its 50th birthday this year) as part of a larger conversation about the way type affects our lives" (*Helvetica* 2007). This document implements a variation of the Helvetica font called Arial.

How we will develop best practices from these results

The literature we reviewed shows that, though some of the basic best practices of communicating have been around for decades, if not centuries, the information design and technical communication disciplines continue to expand knowledge about the nuances of behavior and cognition in reading.

Overall

What is known about readers, information design, and the elements that make up typical print-based communication for hardware and software stems from the shift in focus from the system to the reader that started in the 1960s, the push by the federal government and state agencies to communicate in plain language in the 1970s and 80s, the development of usability testing in the 1990s, and of course the development of computer technology and the Web that expanded access to information in the last 15 years or so.

Approach

Our ultimate goal is to form a solid set of guidelines, based on evidence and best practice, that technical communicators at voting system companies can use to ensure that the documentation they provide as part of their product works efficiently and effectively for the users of the material.

Our final guidelines will incorporate what we learned from reviewing the relevant research literature and from a parallel review of existing style guidelines from various sources.

In an interim step, we will use what we have learned in this phase of the project to assess current voting system documentation and the VVSG guidelines related to documentation. By doing so, we expect to gain an understanding of the gaps between best practices and the communication products that are in use.

We can then focus our proposed guidelines for the VVSG Technical Data Package at the appropriate level of detail for use by our audience, the people who are responsible for developing information products to support voting systems.

References

Alred, Gerald J. 2003. Essential works on technical communication. *Technical Communication* 50 (4): 585-616.

Arditi, Aries and Jianna Cho. 2005. Serifs and font legibility. *Vision Research* 45 (23): 2926-2933.

Bailey, Bob. 2000. Reducing reliance on superstition. *UI Design Newsletter*, September, http://www.humanfactors.com/downloads/sep00.asp# (accessed December 4, 2007).

Bailey, Bob. 2002a. More about fonts. *UI Design Newsletter*, February, http://www.humanfactors.com/downloads/feb02.asp (accessed December 6, 2007).

Bailey, Bob. 2002b. Optimal line length. *UI Design Newsletter*, November, http://www.humanfactors.com/downloads/nov02.asp (accessed December 6, 2007).

Baker, J. Ryan. 2005. Is multiple-column online text better? *Usability News* 7.2. http://psychology.wichita.edu/surl/usabilitynews/72/columns.htm (accessed December 12, 2007).

Bernard, Michael, Chia Hui Liao, and Melissa Mills. 2001. Effects of font type and size on the legibility and reading time of online text by older adults. Paper presented at ACM SIGCHI 2001. http://psychology.wichita.edu/surl/usabilitynews/3W/fontSR.htm (accessed December 12, 2007).

Blakeslee, Ann M., and Rachel Spilka. 2004. The state of research in technical communication. *Technical Communication Quarterly* 13 (1): 73-92.

Boekelder, Angelique, and Michael Steehouder. 1998. Selecting and switching: Some advantages of diagrams over tables and lists for presenting instructions. *IEEE Transactions on Professional Communication* 41 (4): 229-241.

Boekelder, Angelique, and Michael Steehouder. 1999. Switching from instructions to equipment: The effect of graphic design. In *Visual information for everyday use: Design and research perspectives*, ed.

Harm J. G. Zwaga, Theo Boersema, and Henriette C. M. Hoonout, 67-73. London: Taylor and Francis.

Botka, Dana Howard. 2002. From gobbledygook to plain English: How a large state agency took on the bureaucratic form letter. In *Proceedings: STC's 49th Annual Conference.* Society for Technical Communication. http://www.stc.org/ConfProceed/2002/PDFs/STC49-00022.pdf (accessed October 15, 2007).

Brumberger, Eva R. 2003a. The rhetoric of typography: The awareness and impact of typeface appropriateness. *Technical Communication* 50 (2): 224-231.

Brumberger, Eva R. 2003b. The rhetoric of typography: The persona of typeface and text. *Technical Communication* 50 (2): 206-223.

Brumberger, Eva R. 2004. The rhetoric of typography: Effects on reading time, reading comprehension, and perceptions of ethos. *Technical Communication* 51 (1): 13-24.

Burton, Susan. 2007. You may already be a technical communicator! *Intercom*, June, 4.

Carliner, Saul. 2006. Current challenges of research in information and document design. In *Information and document design: Variety on the research*, ed. Saul Carliner, Jan Piet Verckens, and Cathy de Waele, 1-24. Amsterdam, The Netherlands: John Benjamins.

Carroll, John M. 1990. *The Nurnberg Funnel: Designing minimalist instruction for practical computer skill.* Cambridge, MA: MIT Press.

Carroll, John M., ed. 1998. *Minimalism beyond the Nurnberg Funnel.* Cambridge, MA: The MIT Press.

Dixon, Peter. 1987. The processing of organizational and component step information in written directions. *Journal of Memory and Language* 6: 24-35.

Doumont, Jean-luc. 2002. Magical numbers: The seven-plus-or-minus-two myth. *IEEE Transactions on Professional Communication* 45 (2), 123-127.

Farkas, David K. 1999. The logical and rhetorical construction of procedural discourse. *Technical Communication* 46 (1): 42-54.

Felker, Daniel B., Marshall Atlas, Veda R. Charrow, V. Melissa Holland, Cheryl Olkes, Janice C. (Ginny) Redish, and Andrew M. Rose. 1980.

Document design: A review of the relevant research. Washington, DC: American Institutes for Research.

Felker, Daniel B., Frances Pickering, Veda R. Charrow, V. Melissa Holland, and Janice C. (Ginny) Redish. 1981. *Guidelines for document designers*. Washington, DC: American Institutes for Research.

Ganier, Frank. 2004. Factors affecting the processing of procedural instructions: Implications for document design. *IEEE Transactions on Professional Communication* 47 (1): 15-26.

Garvery, Philip M., Martin T. Pietrucha, and Donald Meeker. 1997. Effects of font and capitalization on legibility of guide signs. *Transportation Research Record* 1605: 73-79. http://clearviewhwy.com/ResearchAndDesign/researchWhitepapers.php (accessed December 6, 2007).

Gellevij, Mark, and Hans van der Meij. 2004. Empirical proof for presenting screen captures in software documentation. *Technical Communication* 51 (2): 224-238.

GMAP (Government Management Accountability & Performance). *General guidelines*. Plain Talk, http://www.accountability.wa.gov/plaintalk/ptguidelines/default.asp (accessed December 15, 2007).

Gregory, Judy. 2004. Writing for the web versus writing for print: Are they really so different? *Technical Communication* 51 (2): 276-285.

Hayhoe, George F. 2000. What do technical communicators need to know? *Technical Communication* 47 (2): 151-153.

Helvetica. 2007. Gary Hustwit. London: Swiss Dots.

HHS (Health and Human Services Department). 2006. *Research-Based Web Design & Usability Guidelines*. Usability.gov, http://usability.gov/pdfs/guidelines.html (accessed September 25, 2007).

Hofmann, Patrick. 2004. The successes and challenges of visual language. *Intercom*, June, 16-18.

Horton, William. 1991. *Illustrating computer documentation: The art of presenting information graphically on paper and online*. New York: Wiley.

Isakson, Carol S., and Jan H. Spyridakis. 1999. The influence of semantics and syntax on what readers remember. *Technical Communication* 46 (3): 366-381.

Larson, Kevin. 2004. The science of word recognition or how I learned to stop worrying and love the bouma. Advanced Reading Technology, Microsoft Corporation, http://www.microsoft.com/typography/ctfonts/WordRecognition.aspx (accessed December 6, 2007).

Locke, Joanne. 2004. A history of plain language in the United States government. PlainLanguage.gov, http://www.plainlanguage.gov/whatisPL/history/locke.cfm (accessed November 30, 2007).

Loorbach, Nicole, Joyce Karreman, and Michael Steehouder. 2007. Adding motivational elements to an instruction manual for seniors: Effects on usability and motivation. *Technical Communication* 54 (3): 343-358.

Mazur, Beth. 2000. Revisiting plain language. *Technical Communication* 47 (2): 205-211.

Meeker & Associates. Legibility. ClearviewHwy, http://clearviewhwy.com/ResearchAndDesign/legibilityStudies.php (accessed December 6, 2007).

Miller, George. 1956. The magical number seven, plus or minus two: Some limits on our capacity for processing information. http://www.musanim.com/miller1956 (accessed November 11, 2007). Originally published in *The Psychological Review*, 63 (1956): 81-97.

Mirel, Barbara, and Rachel Spilka. 2002. *Reshaping technical communication: New directions and challenges for the 21st century.* Mahwah, NJ: Lawrence Erlbaum Associates, Inc.

Morkes, John, and Jacob Nielsen. 1997. Concise, SCANNABLE, and objective: How to write for the Web. useit.com: Jakob Nielsen's Website, http://www.useit.com/papers/webwriting/writing.html (accessed November 30, 2007).

Morkes, John, and Jacob Nielsen. 1998. Applying writing guidelines to Web pages. useit.com: Jakob Nielsen's Website, http://www.useit.com/papers/webwriting/rewriting.html (accessed December 4, 2007).

Office of the Federal Register. 1998. Making regulations readable in *Document drafting handbook*, MMR-1-MMR-6. http://www.archives.gov/federal-register/write/plain-language/readable-regulations.pdf (accessed October 17, 2007).

PlainLanguage.gov. Federal plain language guidelines.
http://www.plainlanguage.gov/howto/guidelines/reader-friendly.cfm
(accessed October 15, 2007).

Poole, Alex. 2005. Which are more legible: Serif or sans serif typefaces?
Alex Poole Interaction design and research,
http://www.alexpoole.info/academic/literaturereview.html (accessed
October 4, 2007).

Redish, Janice C. (Ginny). 1988. Reading to learn to do. *Technical
Writing Teacher* 15 (3): 223-233. Reprinted in *IEEE Transactions on
Professional Communication* 32 (1989) (4): 289-293.

Redish, Janice C. (Ginny). 1993. Understanding readers. In *Techniques
for Technical Communicators*, ed. Carol Barnum and Saul Carliner, 14–
41. New York: Macmillan.

Redish, Janice C. (Ginny). 1998. Minimalism in technical communication.
In *Minimalism Beyond the Nurnberg Funnel*, ed. John M. Carroll, 219-
245. Cambridge: The MIT Press.

Redish, Janice C. (Ginny). 2000. What is information design? *Technical
Communication* 47 (2): 163-166.

Redish, Janice C. (Ginny). 2004a. Applying research to practice: What's
relevant today? Presentation at the annual conference of the Society for
Technical Communication, May 9-12, in Baltimore, MD.
http://www.redish.net/content/handouts.html (accessed September 24,
2007).

Redish, Janice C. (Ginny). 2004b. Letting go of the words. *Intercom,*
June, 5-10.

Redish, Janice C. (Ginny). 2006. Guidelines for writing clear instructions
and messages for voters and poll workers. NIST (National Institute of
Standards and Technology),
http://vote.nist.gov/032906PlainLanguageRpt.pdf (accessed September
17, 2007).

Redish, Janice C. (Ginny). 2007. *Letting go of the words*. San Francisco:
Morgan Kaufmann.

Redish, Janice C. (Ginny). Headings. PlainLanguage.gov,
http://www.plainlanguage.gov/howto/guidelines/headings.cfm (accessed
October 15, 2007).

Roebben, Nicolas, and Yves Bestgen. 2006. Reading and expertise: The impact of connectives on text comprehension in the financial field. In *Information and document design: Variety on the research.* Ed. Saul Carliner, Jan Piet Verckens, and Cathy de Waele, 149-165. Amsterdam, The Netherlands: John Benjamins.

Salvo, Michael, Meredith W. Zoetewey, and Kate Agena. 2007. A case of exhaustive documentation: Re-centering system-oriented organizations around user need. *Technical Communication* 54 (1): 46-57.

Schriver, Karen. A. 1997. *Dynamics in document design.* New York: John Wiley & Sons.

Securities and Exchange Commission. 1998. *A plain English handbook: How to create clear SEC disclosure document.* http://www.sec.gov/pdf/handbook.pdf (accessed December 10, 2007).

Spyridakis, Jan H. 2000. Guidelines for authoring comprehensible web pages and evaluating their success. *Technical Communication* 47 (3): 359-382.

Spyridakis, Jan H., Laura D. Schultz, and Alexandra L. Bartell. 2005. Heading frequency and comprehension: Studies of print versus online media. In *Proceedings: STC's 52nd Annual Conference.* Society for Technical Communication. http://www.stc.org/ConfProceed/2005/PDFs/0032.pdf (accessed November 28, 2007).

Spyridakis, Jan H., and Michael J. Wenger. 1992. Writing for human performance: Relating reading research to document design. *Technical Communication* 39 (2): 202-215.

Steehouder, Michael. 2004. Acquiring procedural knowledge of a technology interface: introduction to this special issue. *IEEE Transactions on Professional Communication* 47 (1): 1 – 4.

Steehouder, Michael F., and Carel J. M. Jansen. 1996. The sequential order of instructions: Impact on text quality. In *Proceedings: STC's 43rd Annual Conference.* Society for Technical Communication. http://www.stc.org/confproceed/1996/PDFs/PG247250.PDF (accessed October 04, 2007).

Taylor, Conrad. 2000. Information design: A European perspective. *Technical Communication* 47 (2): 167-168.

van der Meij, Hans, and Mark Gellevij. 1998. Screen captures in software documentation. *Technical Communication* 45 (4): 529-543.

van der Waarde, Karel. 1999. Typographic dimensions and conventional wisdom: A discrepancy? *Technical Communication* 46 (1): 67-74.

Wright, Patricia. 1988. Issues of content and presentation in document design. In *Handbook of human-computer interaction*, ed. M. Helander, 629-652. New York: North-Holland.

Wright, Patricia. 1998. Printed instructions: Can research make a difference? In *Visual information for everyday use: Design and research perspectives*, ed. Harm J. G. Zwaga, Theo Boersema, and Henriette C. M. Hoonout, 45-66. London: Taylor and Francis.

Zimmerman, Donald E. and Terri Prickett. 2000. A usability case study: Prospective students' use of a university web page. In *Proceedings: STC's 47th Annual Conference*. Society for Technical Communication. http://www.stc.org/ConfProceed/2000/PDFs/00099.pdf (accessed December 4, 2007).

Review of relevant literature:
technical communication and information design

Prepared by

UsabilityWorks
453A Chestnut Street
San Francisco, California 94133

Dana E. Chisnell
Susan C. Becker

March, 2008

Contents

Review of relevant literature:
technical communication and information design

Deliverable: A summary review of the literature.

Background

The goal of this project on Voting System Documentation Usability and Poll Worker Usability Testing is to improve the usability of documentation used by poll workers and election support staff by developing these resources:

- Style guide incorporating best practices for voting system documentation

- Protocol for voting system test labs to use to measure the usability of instructions supplied by voting system manufacturers for election workers

The first step in developing the style guide of best practices is this review of relevant information from technical communication and information design literature. Here we review primary and secondary resources that form the thinking behind current best practices in technical communication as they apply to voting systems.

What is technical communication?

"Technical communication is the process of conveying usable information through writing or speech about a specific domain to an intended audience"[13].

When technical communication began to develop in support of the defense and aerospace industries in the decades after World War II, technical writers, like their audiences, were primarily technical experts. In the 1980s and 90s, consumer electronics outpaced these industries as the largest market for technical writing and ordinary people became the largest audience for information products. Since then "the ability to communicate clearly to nonexperts using a variety of media and information types has emerged as the hallmark of technical communication excellence" (Hayhoe 2000, 151).

The Society for Technical Communication (STC), the largest organization in the world dedicated to advancing the arts and sciences of technical communication, today defines technical communicators in part as those who:

> Develop and design instructional and informational tools needed to assure safe, appropriate and effective use of science and technology, intellectual property, and manufactured products and services (Burton 2007).

For our review, we focus on those aspects of technical communication most relevant to developing usable documentation of voting systems; that is, "information tools needed to assure safe, appropriate and effective use" of a manufactured product. We see these information tools primarily as procedures to support setting up voting systems, conducting polling, shutting down voting systems, and auditing voting systems. However, the tools also include descriptions, examples, illustrations, and other types of technical communication.

---

[13] Wikipedia contributors, "Technical communication," *Wikipedia, The Free Encyclopedia*, http://en.wikipedia.org/w/index.php?title=Technical_communication&oldid=175489633 (accessed December 15, 2007).

What we looked for

We looked for sources that discussed the current thinking in best practices in technical communication and information design. We considered primary and secondary sources from technical communication and information design, as well as instructional design, linguistics, reading, cognitive psychology, and human-computer interaction.

Although we focused on sources that used research-based approaches, we also considered those that discuss conventions as well as current trends.

Where we looked

We began by drawing on our experience as practitioners working in technical communication, information architecture, usability testing, instructional design, and teaching, as well as our experience working with NIST and Ginny Redish on the language in instructions on ballots, to create a list of the main research topics in these areas that are especially relevant to writing documentation for voting systems.

We expanded and refined this list by studying other literature reviews and guidelines. In particular, two extensive literature reviews support many of the ideas we cover in this review.

The first, *Document Design: A Review of the Relevant Research* (Felker and others 1980), was developed as part of the Document Design Project, which was funded by the Department of Education. This review and the *Guidelines for Document Designers* (Felker and others 1981) that resulted have provided the basis and set the agenda for much of the discussion in technical communication and document design since the 80s. We used the summaries of early research from these documents in our review.

The second, *Research-Based Web Design & Usability Guidelines* (HHS 2006), developed by the U.S. Department of Health and Human Services (HHS), though not primarily a literature review, includes the over 450 research sources to support its extensive list of guidelines. Although most documentation provided by voting system manufacturers is delivered in print or is meant to be printed, we reviewed the *Research-Based Web Design & Usability Guidelines* as well as other research and guidelines for writing for online presentation and the Web because we believe that they are often relevant to writing for print documentation. (See our discussion of the similarities between writing for print and writing for the web on page 93.) Also, though this review focuses on writing for print, we believe more of the documentation of voting systems will eventually move from print to online presentation.

We reviewed several guidelines from the Plain Language movement, including the *Federal Plain Language Guidelines* (PlainLanguage.gov), *Federal Register Document Drafting Handbook* (Office of the Federal Register 1998), *Washington's Plain Talk Guidelines* (GMAP), and, of course, the *Guidelines for Writing Clear Instructions and Messages for Voters and Poll Workers* (Redish 2006).

We also reviewed several recent works on major directions in research on technical communication written by academics and other researchers in the field; for example, "Current challenges of research in information and document design" (Carliner 2006), "The State of Research in Technical Communication" (Blakeslee and Spilka 2004), and *Reshaping Technical Communication: New Directions and Challenges for the 21st Century* (Mirel and Spilka 2002). These documents helped us determine the role research has played in technical communication and how it may influence future directions.

All of these sources helped us determine the basic theories of technical communication that people working or doing research in the field generally agree upon today. From these sources, we followed up many of the references we found in those studies, articles, and books that support the theories. We supplemented our sources by searching on the Internet (Google, Google Scholar) and in online libraries and newsletters (ACM Digital Library, Ingenta, Human Factors International, EServer Technical Communication Library).

How we dealt with the quantity of available resources

The challenge we faced in writing a review of the literature and research that pertains to technical communication and information design in the 21st century is the quantity of research generated over the past sixty years, and especially since 1980.

For example, Alred's 2003 "Essential Works on Technical Communication" presents an annotated list of 115 essential works compiled from a list of over 600 titles. One of those, *The St. Martin's bibliography of business and technical communication* includes 376 works (Alred 2003).

The authors of the 2006 *Research-Based Web Design & Usability Guidelines* at usability.gov reduced their initial 500 guidelines to the current 187, but those are based on over 450 listed resources. A panel of 18 experts assigned "Strength of Evidence" ratings for the guidelines.

Within the scope of this review, we could not read all the sources that we wanted to use. Though we do include several primary sources, we have also relied on secondary sources and on their summaries of other primary and secondary sources.

What we found

As might be expected, although some early directions in technical communication have become less important as technology has evolved, most have continued to be developed and refined by more recent research. And of course new ideas are developing.

In this review, we focus on the issues that we believe are the most helpful in improving and assuring the usability of the documentation of voting systems. We cover major concepts that have been generally accepted since the 1980s (for example, the use of common words rather than jargon) as well as major issues that have been developing since then (such as skimming and scanning behavior in reading), and especially in more recent years (for example, the use of screenshots in software documentation).

The review focuses on the following issues:

How Information and document design continue to evolve

- Plain language movement made government documents clearer
- Technological advances broaden the definition of document design
- Information design and document design are merging
- Plain language, usability are gaining momentum
- Writing for print and writing for the web are similar

What we know about readers and users

- People use manuals to find the information they need to do their work
- Readers skim and scan information rather than reading carefully
- Readers interpret as they read and act on the first reasonable option
- Setting the context helps users understand and complete instructions
- People can process only a limited amount of information at a time
- Readers comprehend more when the topic is interesting or familiar

What we know about information design

- Documents that are user-oriented are easier to comprehend
- Headings and other "signals" help readers comprehend text
- Information presented in a logical order is easier to understand
- Information presented first is easier to remember

What we know about words, sentences and paragraphs

- Common words and short words are easier to understand
- Short, simple sentences are easier to comprehend and remember

What we know about graphics and illustrations

- Graphics are understood more quickly than words
- Graphics and text together are more effective than words
- Graphics help users decide when to switch from instructions to a task
- Screenshots help users comprehend documentation

What we know about typography

- Mixed-case is easier to read than all upper case
- Emphasizing text helps but too much emphasis can be distracting
- Serif and sans serif are equally legible
- Leading and line length affect legibility
- Ragged right alignment is preferred by document designers
- Typefaces have emotional content

Information and document design continue to evolve

- Plain language movement made government documents clearer
- Technological advances broaden the definition of document design
- Information design and document design are merging
- Plain language, usability are gaining momentum
- Writing for print and writing for the web are similar

Plain language movement made government documents clearer

In the 1960s and especially the 1970s, the plain language movement in the United States, supported by Presidents Nixon and Carter, worked to make government documents easier for the citizens who used them to understand (Carliner 2006; Locke 2004; Schriver 1997). Other countries have also been involved in the plain language movements for even longer than the US (Locke 2004; Mazur 2000; Schriver 1997).

One result was the Document Design Project, which studied the problems of public documents and helped agencies implement plain language. It created *Document Design: A Review of the Relevant Research* and the *Guidelines for Document Designers*, which served as a handbook for government writers for many years (Locke 2004).

However, President Reagan rescinded President Carter's Executive Orders, and within the Federal Government, the plain language movement made limited progress during the 1980s (Locke 2004).

Although the research community supported government action to improve writing, there was some discussion about its definition of the audience and its methods for evaluating documents.[14] By the mid-1980s, the research community replaced studies in plain language with "more broadly conceived efforts in document design [which] examined readers' actual comprehension and use of documents" as well as their responses to visual language (Schriver 1997, 29).

Technological advances broaden the definition of document design

The technological advances of the 1980s, which included the first practical personal computers and desktop publishing, also changed the way documents were produced and the nature of documents themselves (Schriver 1997). Researchers (and technical writers) worked to understand the most effective ways to communicate with the new

---

[14] Mazur (2000) refutes these criticisms of plain language in a discussion of its past and current resources.

technology, while also beginning to look at ways to make documents more usable (Carliner 2006).

As web technology exploded in the 1990s, technical communicators were joined by other information providers in developing ways to organize and present information online. In particular, those with a background in library science developed the concepts of information architecture, which is concerned with organizing and labeling websites and other online environments to support usability.

Information design and document design are merging

For technical communication, two concepts continue to be central: document design and information design. Some technical communicators make a distinction between these, defining document design as the way information is presented (layout, typography, color, and so on) and information design as the "overall process of developing a successful document" (Redish 2000, 163).

For example, Carliner (2006) distinguishes between the two:

> Document design focuses on providing readers with physical markers that help them find content of interest and with the general appearance of information so it is both pleasing and usable (2).

> Information design takes a broader perspective, focusing on the meaning-making of text…specifically…preparing communication products so that they achieve the performance objectives established for them (2-3).

Schriver (1997) defines document design as "a field concerned with creating texts (broadly defined) that integrate words and pictures in ways that help people to achieve their specific goals for using texts at home, school, or work (10)."

Others, including Redish (2000), use information design to describe both the overall process and the presentation of information on the page or screen. And Carliner (2006) concedes that the two terms are merging as indicated by the merging of the *Information Design Journal* and *Document Design* into a single journal.[15]

For our purposes, we generally use the terms interchangeably and note that technical communication is now concerned with both information

---

[15] The European tradition of information design involves a broader scope, "to improve the design of information artifacts and systems encountered by people in every part of their daily lives," such as wayfinding in museums and other public places, not just documentation (Taylor 2000, 167).

design and document design, and how they relate to each other (Redish 2000).

Plain language, usability are gaining momentum

In 1998, President Clinton, in a memorandum that requires all new federal regulations to be written in plain language, stated:

> Plain language documents have logical organization; common, everyday words, except for necessary technical terms; 'you' and other pronouns; the active voice; and short sentences (Locke 2004).

Clinton's description reaffirms many of the basic ideas of plain language as well as good information design.

In 1998, the Securities and Exchange Commission published *A Plain English Handbook: How to create clear SEC disclosure documents*, which "remains an excellent resource on plain language writing" (Locke 2004).[16]

In 2001, the Washington State Department of Labor and Industries started "Plain Talk," a project to rewrite their form letters in Plain English (Botka 2002). The project was so successful that in 2005, Governor Christine O. Gregoire issued an executive order that all agencies adopt the principles and practices of Plain Talk.

In the current decade, several other movements in technical communication have gained momentum: the role of usability research in document design, the Internet as a means of delivering content, and research-based heuristics, such as the *Research-Based Web Design & Usability Guidelines* at www.usability.gov (Carliner 2006).

Writing for print and writing for the web are similar

Many of the discussions of writing for the web in the workplace started with the premise that writing for the web was different from writing for print, that it needed to be clearer, more concise, more aware of chunking, organized more clearly with precise headings, links and navigation.

But Gregory (2004) presents arguments to show that many of the underlying principles of writing apply to both print and online and have a long history in writing for print. For example, the suggestion that web authors should provide 50% less content is similar to the basic guidelines for Plain Language to have fewer words and shorter sentences. The idea

---

[16] Many US federal agencies have plain-language programs, including the Federal Aviation Administration, the Federal Register, the Food and Drug Administration, Health and Human Services, National Institutes of Health, and Veteran's Benefits Administration (Locke 2004).

that readers skim, which is the basis for writing scannable text, applies to both online and print, as does the idea that readers go directly to the information they need rather than reading cover-to-cover or from the top. The importance of "chunking" information, which is a common guideline for web writing, has been discussed as dividing information into coherent sections at least since the Document Design Project in 1980.

Similarly, Spyridakis (2000) found in her review that researchers in the 1980s believed that print documents and hypertext were significantly different in that print documents were linear, but hypertext documents were not. But more recent research showed that the two media are similar, that readers move around in both and then read when they locate the information they want.

Spyridakis (2000) also found that research in the 1980s and 90s, on how the medium (paper versus online) affects reading comprehension and recall, were not conclusive: some found better performance with print, some with online, and some with neither.

Of course, there is a danger in using research based on a context, on a specific communications challenge, to create more universal heuristic guidelines. Some researchers question whether results of research can be generalized from one population to another, from print-based to online or online to print, or from a single publication to any document (Carliner 2006). Carliner (2006) points out that we have "a need for more specific guidelines on communication than the research currently provides" (13). However, despite its shortcomings, research and theory based on research can provide a corrective (or at least augment) for what Brumberger (2004) calls, in speaking of typography, "the practitioners' lore and intuition" (13).

What we know about readers and users

- People use manuals to find the information they need to do their work

- Readers skim and scan information rather than reading carefully

- Readers interpret as they read and act on the first reasonable option

- Setting the context helps users understand and complete instructions

- People can process only a limited amount of information at a time

- Readers comprehend more when the topic is interesting or familiar

People use manuals to find the information they need to do their work

"In daily life, people do not follow all the instructions that they encounter, only those relating to the goals that they currently have" (Wright 1998, 52).

Users of software and hardware are focused on their own task and are seldom in a learning or study mode. They turn to manuals to find what they need in order to accomplish their immediate goal and then get back to it. They are usually "reading to do" when they turn to manuals, rather than reading to learn or even reading to learn to do (Redish 1998, 1993, 1988).

Users turn to manuals when:

- They don't know what tasks they need to complete to reach a goal.

- They don't know the steps for a specific task.

- They have a problem, whether they can state it clearly or not (Redish 1998).

Schriver (1997) found that, of the users that she surveyed, only 23% reported that they read the instructions before they tried a new function, 42% said they read the instructions while they tried the new function, 17% said they referred to the instructions only when they were confused, and 19% said they did not use the instructions at all.

Readers seldom go to manuals for conceptual information (Redish 1998).

Wright says that the questions people ask of technical information are problem-driven ("Why didn't that work?") or task-driven ("How do I do that?"). They are not usually system-driven ("How does it work?") (Redish 1998, 20).[17]

---

[17] Redish is referring to Patricia Wright (1988).

Readers skim and scan information rather than reading carefully

The idea that readers scan has appeared in discussions of technical writing frequently since 1981 (Gregory 2004). Readers of both print and online documents scan information rather than reading it thoroughly (Redish 2004b).

Schriver (1997) found that roughly 80% of the consumers she surveyed reported that they scanned their instruction manuals or used them as a reference—46% of the users said they scanned them; 35% said they used the documents for reference (they went to a specific page to get a specific piece of information).

Studies of how people read on the Web found that they also scan and that sites that are more scannable are easier to use. A study of five different writing styles found that a sample Web site scored 47% higher in measured usability when it was designed to be scannable; that is, it had bulleted lists, boldface text to highlight key words, photo captions, shorter sections of text, and more headings than the control site. Users performed tasks faster, made fewer errors, and recalled the content of the site better (Morkes and Nielsen 1997).

Readers interpret as they read and act on the first reasonable option

Research shows that people tend to act as soon as they see something that talks about action. They do not wait to finish the sentence if the context for that action is at the end of the sentence. They do not read to the end of a paragraph even if a caution about the action comes later in the paragraph (Carroll 1990; Redish 1988, 1993).

Carroll (1990) observed that users tended to act before reading instructions. He describes the paradox of sense making that users of a new program face: To interact meaningfully with a new program, users need to acquire certain skills and understanding. But they can acquire these only through meaningful interaction with the program. Faced with this paradox, users tend to pick the first reasonable action rather than learn all possible actions and pick the best.

People reading voting machine documentation also act in this way, especially poll workers on Election Day who are under pressure to keep the voters moving through the polling place.

Setting the context helps users understand and complete instructions

On the sentence level, readers also act as soon as they see a reasonable option, even if their initial interpretation might be incorrect. Research shows that when the general organizational information comes first, readers understand directions more easily and they make fewer mistakes (Dixon 1987). That is, when the context is set before the action, readers can follow directions more successfully.

Dixon (1987) investigated what people did with instructions that had two parts, general organizational information (context) and component step information (actions), depending on the order of the parts.

This is an example from the study, with the context first:

> This will be a picture of a wine glass.
> Draw a triangle on top of an upside-down T.

This is an example with the action first:

> Draw a triangle on top of an upside-down T.
> This will be a picture of a wine glass.

Dixon was especially interested in what the readers would do when the action came first: would they hold the information in memory until they had the context, or would they guess the context and act immediately. The results showed that they guessed and did not wait. When the context came first, most readers drew a wine glass; when the action came first, many drew a Christmas tree.[18]

Dixon theorized that users sometimes make errors in following directions because they misinterpret how the steps are organized and work together. He suggested that "the problem could be alleviated by providing initially some high-level information about the nature and organization of the task" (Dixon 1987, 33). That is, some context.

Brief overviews, such as lists of headings, graphics, flowcharts, or short sets of questions and answers, help users understand instructions (Redish 1998). Redish and Dumas also showed that providing this type of information, even in a manual that users turn to only when they need to find information to complete a task, helps them learn (Redish 1998).

Poll workers who are setting up voting machines under stressful conditions (early hours, an unfamiliar setting, time pressure, a machine they may have never seen before) may easily misinterpret directions, especially if they simply follow step-by-step instructions that do not provided them with a context.

---

[18] Thanks to Sharon J. Laskowski and Ginny Redish, for this framing of Dixon's work in their presentation *Making Ballot Language Understandable to Voters* (Laskowski and Redish 2006).

People can process only a limited amount of information at a time

Miller (1956) first showed that short-term or working memory is limited in the number of elements it can contain simultaneously. According to a model Ganier (2004) discusses, "cognitive processes involved in the processing of instructions occur in working memory, which is constrained in both time and processing capacity" (16).

When readers need to remember more information than they can handle in their working memory while performing a procedure, they experience a "cognitive load" which can lead to errors (Steehouder and Jansen 1996).

Cognitive psychology has shown that people use a strategy of grouping or organizing information into chunks to increase the amount of information they can hold in short-term memory (Miller 1956).[19]

Chunking, which is discussed extensively in guidelines for writing for online presentation, is also an important technique in writing documentation for print (Redish 1993; Gregory 2004). In technical writing and information design literature, "chunking" refers to breaking text into short pieces, often with meaningful headings. Research that Spyridakis and Wenger (1992) reviewed showed that chunking decreases the demands on the reader's memory and improves comprehension.

Many procedure writers also follow the short-term memory rule-of-thumb that the length of a list should be no more than seven, plus or minus two, based on Miller (1956) *Psychology Review* article. But analysis of Miller's article since then has shown that seven is not the "magical number" he thought it to be (Doumont 2002). Bailey (2000) reports that various researchers have suggested the working memory capacity is actually four to six items, four items, or three items.

But considering that people read to do and once they have found an actionable instruction move to perform it, the limits of working memory do not need to limit the length of a list of procedures. There is no expectation that the audience needs to memorize the list even for a short time.

---

[19] "In cognitive psychology and mnemonics, chunking refers to a strategy for making more efficient use of short-term memory by recoding information. More generally, Herbert Simon has used the term chunk to indicate long-term memory structures that can be used as units of perception and meaning, and chunking as the learning mechanisms leading to the acquisition of these chunks." Wikipedia contributors. Chunking (psychology). *Wikipedia, The Free Encyclopedia.* http://en.wikipedia.org/wiki/Chunking_%28psychology%29 (accessed December 4, 2007).

Readers comprehend more when the topic is interesting or familiar

Research shows that "readers comprehend better and retain more information when they are interested in the topic of the passage" (Isakson and Spyridakis 1999, 367).

Isakson and Spyridakis (1999) found in their research that "readers recall information they perceive to be more important more frequently than information they perceive to be less important" (377). A recent study on motivational elements in instruction manuals for seniors found that adding motivational elements improved task performance (Loorbach, Joyce, and Steehouder 2007).

Research also shows that prior knowledge can assist comprehension, although one study showed prior knowledge had no effect (Isakson and Spyridakis 1999).

Cognitive psychology teaches us that "users construct their own mental models (schemas), combining new information from what they see in interfaces and documentation with what they already have in their minds from earlier experiences" (Redish 1998, 220). Prior knowledge can help users understand and incorporate new information more quickly. But it can also result in their jumping to conclusions about the new information, trying to match it to their existing mental models which may not be appropriate (Carroll 1990).

What we know about information design

- Documents that are user-oriented are easier to comprehend

- Headings and other "signals" help readers comprehend text

- Information presented in a logical order is easier to understand

- Information presented first is easier to remember

Documents that are user-oriented are easier to comprehend

Carroll (1990) in his work on minimalism in instructional design found that instructional manuals based on users' tasks were more effective than those based on a comprehensive presentation of system-related tasks. Carroll argues that you cannot design training "that is both usable and comprehensive" (93). The goal of minimalism is "to teach people what they need to learn in order to do what they wish to do" (Carroll 1990, 3) rather than trying to teach them a conceptual model of how the system works.

Redish (1998) reaffirmed the importance of focusing on the user in her argument for a user-centered process for documentation: "Extensive, iterative interactions with users and making sure of what is learned in those interactions is critical to successful documentation" (236).

Salvo, Zoetewey, and Agena (2007) showed that product documentation that is system oriented and written without consideration of how it would be used or under what circumstances "can be overwhelming for target-audience end users" as well as expensive for manufacturers (48).

Schriver (1997) demonstrated that it is critical to consider the readers' thoughts and feelings when designing documents that inform or persuade. When the document designers did not take the real readers seriously, the documents were ineffective even when the readers could comprehend them. In addition, the image of the organization behind the documents suffered. "Failing to consider the knowledge and values of the real audience can create a lasting negative identity for the organization that may take years to shake" (204).

With voter confidence already low, documentation of voting systems needs to be user-centered not only to help poll workers use the machines to accomplish their tasks, but also to convey an image of the voting system manufacturers as people who are concerned about making voting run smoothly on Election Day and providing fair results. User-centered documents can do both more effectively than system-centered documentation.

Headings and other "signals" help readers comprehend text

Research shows that when readers encounter "signals" in print text, they are able to better comprehend new or difficult information. "These signals—headings, summaries, overview sentences, and other types of cues about text content—help readers create…a structural and content-based context that helps readers take in new information" (Spyridakis, Schultz, and Bartell 2005, 138).

Headings help users determine where they are in a document and a task. They help users orient themselves and make the right associations with their pre-existing concepts or schemas (Redish 2004a). Research shows that headings also "provide clues about information importance" (Spyridakis, Schultz, and Bartell 2005, 138) and they help people find information faster (Redish on PlainLanguage.gov). Perhaps for that reason, they are important in making text scannable in online documents (Morkes and Nielsen 1997).

People also prefer that documents have headings. They believe that documents with headings are easier to read and understand, and they are more motivated to use them (Redish on PlainLanguage.gov).

To be effective, headings need to focus on the users' tasks, not the system (Redish 1998). Headings need to "make connections to the user." Nouns and noun phrases are not as effective as questions and phrases that include verbs and people, for example, personal pronouns (Redish on PlainLanguage.gov).

Good headings help users form a goal and monitor their progress toward it. Users are able to process instructions more efficiently if they are given precise headings that correspond to their goals (Ganier 2004). For example, if the poll worker's goal is to override an error and accept a voter's ballot as is, a heading might be "Accepting a voter's ballot when there is an error message" or "Overriding an error message when a voter requests it."

Causal connectives (for example, *because*) are another type of signal. Roebben and Bestgen (2006) showed that when causal connectives were included in texts "low expertise level readers as well as high expertise level readers learned more from coherent texts (with connectives) than less coherent text (without connectives)" (149).

Information presented in a logical order is easier to understand

Information that is presented in a logical order is easier for the readers to understand. This is especially true for series of steps in a procedure. In particular, time-based sequences are easily understood by users.

Research shows that "the sequence of verbal information can determine how information is stored in memory and retrieved" and that randomly or arbitrarily reordering sentences decreased learning (Felker and others 1980, 56).

Steehouder and Jansen (2004) argue that "the sequential order of procedural steps is crucial for effective and efficient performance." They describe three "rules" for optimizing instructions:

- First things first: put instructions in an order that prevents users from neglecting important steps.

- Minimize cognitive load: put instructions in an order that allows readers to forget what they read.

- Save time and effort: put instructions in an order that "on average" requires as little time as possible of the readers. (247)

Information presented first is easier to remember

Research shows that readers recall information better when it is presented first (primacy) or last (recency) in lists rather than in the middle of lists. One study of prose found that recall of propositions in text was highest from first to last to middle in two of eight passages. Another prose study found only primacy effects. Yet another study found both primacy and recency effects (Isakson and Spyridakis 1999).

These studies indicate that information presented last is also easier to remember. However, as we discussed, readers interpret as they read and respond to the first reasonable option. So we believe that, under normal circumstances, the recall of the last item is not relevant.

Dixon (1987) also notes that procedural directions are read faster when general organizational information is found at the beginning rather than at the end of directions.

What we know about words, sentences and paragraphs

- Common words and short words are easier to understand

- Short, simple sentences are easier to comprehend and remember

Common words and short words are easier to understand

The seminal texts on Document Design, *Document Design: A Review of Relevant Research* (Felker and others 1980) and *Guidelines for Document Designers* (Felker and others 1981), cite studies and reviews of studies that support these ideas:

- Less frequent and harder words take longer to recognize.

- Harder words are harder to remember.

- Sentences and text containing harder words take longer to read and reading takes more effort.

- Sentences with harder words take longer to use.

- Concrete words are easier to learn and recall than abstract words.

Spyridakis has discussed additional research before and since 1980 that shows that high-frequency words (words that are used frequently in the English language) and short words are easier for readers to recognize and comprehend than their low-frequency or longer counterparts (Spyridakis 2000; Isakson and Spyridakis 1999; Spyridakis and Wenger 1992).

Spyridakis also notes additional research showing that "words that represent concrete concepts are encoded more quickly and accurately, recalled more often, and comprehended better than words that represent abstract concepts" (Spyridakis 2000, 368).

A more recent study found that perspective students in a usability test of university websites had difficulty using the sites because they did not understand the universities' terminology and jargon (Zimmerman and Prickett 2000).

Common words and short words may be easier to read because of the way we recognize words. Evidence from the last 20 years of work in cognitive psychology indicates that readers use the letters within a word to recognize a word. "We recognize a word's component letters, then use that visual information to recognize a word. In addition to perceptual information, we also use contextual information to help recognize words during ordinary reading" (Larson 2004).

Short, simple sentences are easier to comprehend and remember

Felker and others (1981), in *Guidelines for Document Designers*, cited studies that show that short sentences are easier to read and understand. They also noted other factors that can affect comprehension, including whether a sentence is concrete or abstract, grammatically complex, or sparse or dense with information. They concluded that, although the length of the sentence is important, "it is not sufficient in itself to ensure that the sentence will be easy to understand" (43).

Syntax (the way words are grammatically formed and ordered to form phrases, clauses, and sentences) can affect comprehension and recall.

Research in the 1970s and 80s showed that readers recall independent clauses faster than clauses that cannot stand alone as a sentence (dependent clauses). Readers also showed poorer comprehension of important information in dependent clauses than of important information in independent clauses (Isakson and Spyridakis 1999).

Embedded clauses (clauses inside other clauses, often seen after relative pronouns like who, that, or which) can also cause problems (Redish 2004a). Research shows that readers make more comprehension errors with relative clauses that are embedded in the middle of a sentence than they do with those at the end of a sentence (Isakson and Spyridakis 1999; Spyridakis and Wenger 1992).

Isakson and Spyridakis (1999) found that readers were more likely to recall information when it was in clauses (rather than phrases or other structures) or independent clauses (rather than dependent clauses, relative clauses, or other structures). Readers also recalled information in relative clauses that were at the end of the sentence better than in relative clauses embedded in the middle of the sentence. But the researchers were not sure whether that was because of the location of the relative clause or of the information itself at the end of the sentence.

Two studies of Web sites by Morkes and Nielsen (1997, 1998) showed that Web sites with concisely written text were more usable. The 1997 study of different writing styles found that a sample Web site scored 58% higher in measured usability when it was written concisely; that is, written with much shorter text. The combined version, which was written concisely, written for scannability, and stripped of "marketese," scored 124% higher in measured usability.

In the 1998 study, Morkes and Nielsen redesigned a Web site following writing guidelines to make the site "concise, easy to scan, and objective (rather than promotional) in style." They report that "the rewritten website scored 159% higher than the original in measured usability."

What we know about graphics and illustrations

- Graphics are understood more quickly than words

- Graphics and text together are more effective than words

- Graphics help users decide when to switch from instructions to a task

- Screenshots help users comprehend documentation

Graphics are understood more quickly than words

According to models of picture and text comprehension, we process pictures and text differently. Building a mental model from text requires more resources and so creates a heavier cognitive load than building a mental model from pictures (Ganier 2004).[20]

When people use instructions to operate a new piece of equipment, adding pictures can "reduce the cognitive load and enhance the elaboration of a mental model" because of the similarity of the picture and the equipment and perhaps the user's internal representations (Ganier 2004, 21).

Pictures are often easier to remember than verbal descriptions (Horton 1991; Felker and others 1980, 35).

Graphics and text together are more effective than words

Research prior to 1980 showed that graphics, including pictures, drawings, graphs, flowcharts, and tables, are often better than text at making certain kinds of relationships clear. One study found that the most appropriate presentation depends on the nature and difficulty of the problem. For example, "tables are the quickest for solving easy problems, if the user knows what to look for," but "flowcharts are the most accurate, especially if the user does not know what to look for, or if the problem is hard." The study also found that "bureaucratic prose…yields the slowest and least-accurate problem solving" (Felker and others 1981, 35).

Since the 1980s, more studies have shown that using a mixed format of text and pictures leads to better performance than just text or pictures alone (Ganier 2004; Gellevij and van der Meij 2004).

Boekelder and Steehouder (1998) tested the effects of instructions that were presented in prose steps, a decision table, a flowchart, a logical

---

[20] "According to [current models of text and picture comprehension], text would lead to the construction of internal verbal representations and then to propositional representations that would allow the user to build a situational or a mental model. In contrast, a picture is considered as an external model (an analogical visual representation) that allows a more direct construction of a mental model." (Ganier 2004, 21)

tree, or a yes/no tree. The study showed that performance was best with a flowchart, logical tree, or yes/no tree, and worst with prose steps or decision table. The study also showed that the participants generally preferred the format they were used to (the one they used during the study), even when it was not the most effective, with the exception of the prose format. They preferred any graphical format to prose.

Interestingly, Boekelder and Steehouder (1998) did not include a continuous prose version because of the "unanimous results of the experiments reported in the literature. Graphical formats proved to be more effective and efficient than prose in all experiments" (234).

Hoffman (2004) describes a project in which he and his colleagues developed a "wordless" installation manual for a network computer. The manual, which was produced for a global audience, provided instructions with illustrations only. Navigation within a document (the table of contents) and between documents was also provided by illustrations. Usability testing and customer surveys indicated that the documentation was successful, especially in the eastern Asian market.

Graphics help users decide when to switch from instructions to a task

When users of hardware and software turn to a manual for information to complete a task, they do not read an entire procedure and then act on it, but instead switch from the text to the equipment and then back, if they need more information. The user decides when to switch one way or the other, though generally, the best time to switch is right after reading a single step (Boekelder and Steehouder 1998). From this we also conclude that writing steps that contain just one action could facilitate switching at the best time.

Boekelder and Steehouder (1999) showed that when sentences were ruled or boxed off (that is, when a line appeared across the page after each sentence) readers switched from reading to action at that point more often than when the lines were not there. Readers did this even when it was not the best time to do so; for example, when more than one action was included in a box, readers postponed the action until they read the whole box.

Screenshots help users comprehend documentation

Gellevij and van der Meij (2004) showed that users benefit from screen captures (screenshots) in software documentation. Screen captures when combined with text help the user:

- Develop a mental model of the way the program works and how it is structured

- Identify and locate window elements and objects

- Verify screen states and so recover from errors

Gellevij and van der Meij (2004) also believed that screenshots can help users determine when to switch between the documentation and the screen. But the study showed that users switched appropriately whether the documentation included screen captures or not. Gellevij and van der Meij suggest that their users already had a good basic "switching mode."[21]

---

[21] In a previous article, van der Meij and Gellevij (1998) provide an in-depth review of the literature and discuss the functions of screen captures that their 2004 study confirms.

What we know about typography

- Mixed-case is easier to read than all upper case

- Emphasizing text helps but too much emphasis can be distracting

- Serif and sans serif are equally legible

- Leading and line length affect legibility

- Ragged right alignment is preferred by document designers

- Typefaces have emotional content

Mixed-case is easier to read than all upper case

Research shows that reading speed is optimal when uppercase and lower case letters are used. Reading speed is slower when text is all capital letters (Schriver 1997; Felker and others 1981).[22]

Although its relationship with printed documentation may be tenuous, Clearview-Condensed, a font developed for road signs provides some additional arguments against using all capital letters. The developers of the font found that when the upper/lowercase Clearview-Condensed was compared to the most commonly used all-capital-letter typeface, "there was a 14 percent increase in recognition when viewed by older drivers at night, with no loss of legibility. When the size of Clearview-Condensed was increased by 12 percent to equal the overall footprint of the uppercase display, the recognition gain doubled to 29 percent with little change in overall sign size" (Meeker & Associates; Garvery, Pietrucha, and Meeker 1997).

Emphasizing text helps but too much emphasis can be distracting

Research reviewed by Felker and others (1981) shows that emphasizing specific information in text, using typographic clues, such as bolding, italics, font style, font size, and case, can help readers understand and remember the information. The research shows that readers understand and remember highlighted information better. However, combining techniques or overusing them can be confusing for the reader. The research also shows that **bold** is a better way to show emphasis than UPPERCASE.

Serif and sans serif are equally legible

Reviews of the research literature by Poole (2005), Bailey (2002a), and Schriver (1997) show that serif and sans serif fonts are equally legible A

---

[22] Reading lower case text faster is the result of practice; most readers spend most of their time reading lower case text and so are better at it (Larson 2004). However, we believe that this will most likely continue to be the case.

study by Arditi and Cho (2005) found "no difference in legibility between typefaces that differ only in the presence or absence of serifs" (1).

Though an earlier study reviewed by Schriver (1997) found serif and sans serif fonts equally preferred, Bailey (2002a) concluded from his review, that "most users tend to prefer sans serif fonts."

When testing online fonts, Bernard, Liao, and Mills (2001) found an effect for type size when they compared reading efficiency between serif and sans serif type fonts with 27 adults between the ages of 62 and 83. Overall, participants read 14-point type faster than 12-point type. When given a choice, participants also preferred 14-point type over 12-point type. However, Bernard and his team found that participants read the 14-point serif type fastest. (One untested theory is that the participants in Bernard's study may have read serif type faces fastest because they are accustomed to reading newsprint, whereas younger adults may be more accustomed to reading text in other media which tend to use sans serif typefaces.)

Leading and line length affect legibility

Research on how line length affects reading speed has been going on since 1881—over 125 years! Early research in 1881, 1883, and 1929, set the optimal length between 3 and 4 inches (Bailey 2002b).

For about the last fifty years, research and typographic guidelines have suggested an optimum line length of 10 to 12 words per line, or about 50 to 70 characters, for most conventional type sizes (9 to 12 points) (Felker and others 1981; Shriver 1997).

Typography experts hesitate to make guidelines about line length and when they do they tend to disagree (Shriver 1997). And actual practice does not always reflect the suggested guidelines (van der Waarde 1999). But in general, designers of instruction guides lean toward the lower end of the recommendation (8 or 9 words a line).

Leading refers to the space between lines. Leading interacts with type size and line length, so for example, large type usually requires more leading. Research reviewed by Shriver (1997) shows that readers dislike type that has either no space between lines (is "set solid") or too much leading (4 points of leading with 10-point type) and people read faster when the text is set to 1 to 4 points of leading than when text is set solid.

Guidelines usually reflect these findings, but as with line length, they are not always followed in general practice (van der Waarde 1999).

Research on the affects of line length on reading speed and comprehension on the web shows that

> Longer line lengths typically result in faster reading times, but research suggests medium to short line lengths typically may result in higher comprehension. In terms of columnar text, the research supports both long single columns of text, and multiple short columns while preference seems to lie towards multiple short columns (Baker 2005).

Ragged right alignment is preferred by document designers

Ragged right (flush left) text is aligned on the left margin with a ragged right margin like this report. Justified text is aligned along the left margin, and letter- and word-spacing is adjusted so that the text is also flush with the right margin.

Research reviewed by Felker and all (1981) and Schriver (1997) shows little difference in reading comprehension between ragged right text and justified text, except possibly for slow readers.

However, justified text can have unequal spaces between words that can create "rivers" or paths of blank space running vertically through the text. Rivers can affect reading speed negatively (Schriver 1997). But generally ragged right alignment is used because it is preferred by document designers.

Baker (2005) examined how multiple columns and text justification affect online reading of a narrative passage in terms of reading speed, comprehension, and satisfaction. He found that fast readers did best with two-column full-justified text and slow readers did best with a single column of non-justified text.

This research of text alignment of both print and online documents suggests that ragged-right is the most appropriate for poll workers. Whether poll workers are fast or slow readers, we believe they would function more like slow readers, in the environment of Election Day at the polls.

Typefaces have emotional content

Brumberger (2004, 2003a, 2003b), through extensive work on the rhetoric of typography, found that readers perceive typefaces and text to have personality attributes. Readers can also determine if typefaces are appropriate or inappropriate for a particular text (for example, a "direct" font like Arial is appropriately used for a professional text or inappropriately used for a "friendly text").

However, in Brumberger's study the persona of the typeface did not have a significant impact on reading comprehension or reading time. Also, the font did not change the reader's perception of the text; that is, a "friendly" font did not make the readers think the document was "friendly."

For a less theoretical treatment of the emotional content and impact of typefaces, see *Helvetica*, the feature-length independent film about typography, graphic design and global visual culture. "It looks at the proliferation of one typeface (which is celebrating its 50th birthday this year) as part of a larger conversation about the way type affects our lives" (*Helvetica* 2007). This document implements a variation of the Helvetica font called Arial.

How we will develop best practices from these results

The literature we reviewed shows that, though some of the basic best practices of communicating have been around for decades, if not centuries, the information design and technical communication disciplines continue to expand knowledge about the nuances of behavior and cognition in reading.

Overall

What is known about readers, information design, and the elements that make up typical print-based communication for hardware and software stems from the shift in focus from the system to the reader that started in the 1960s, the push by the federal government and state agencies to communicate in plain language in the 1970s and 80s, the development of usability testing in the 1990s, and of course the development of computer technology and the Web that expanded access to information in the last 15 years or so.

Approach

Our ultimate goal is to form a solid set of guidelines, based on evidence and best practice, that technical communicators at voting system companies can use to ensure that the documentation they provide as part of their product works efficiently and effectively for the users of the material.

Our final guidelines will incorporate what we learned from reviewing the relevant research literature and from a parallel review of existing style guidelines from various sources.

In an interim step, we will use what we have learned in this phase of the project to assess current voting system documentation and the VVSG guidelines related to documentation. By doing so, we expect to gain an understanding of the gaps between best practices and the communication products that are in use.

We can then focus our proposed guidelines for the VVSG Technical Data Package at the appropriate level of detail for use by our audience, the people who are responsible for developing information products to support voting systems.

References

Alred, Gerald J. 2003. Essential works on technical communication. *Technical Communication* 50 (4): 585-616.

Arditi, Aries and Jianna Cho. 2005. Serifs and font legibility. *Vision Research* 45 (23): 2926-2933.

Bailey, Bob. 2000. Reducing reliance on superstition. *UI Design Newsletter*, September, http://www.humanfactors.com/downloads/sep00.asp# (accessed December 4, 2007).

Bailey, Bob. 2002a. More about fonts. *UI Design Newsletter*, February, http://www.humanfactors.com/downloads/feb02.asp (accessed December 6, 2007).

Bailey, Bob. 2002b. Optimal line length. *UI Design Newsletter*, November, http://www.humanfactors.com/downloads/nov02.asp (accessed December 6, 2007).

Baker, J. Ryan. 2005. Is multiple-column online text better? *Usability News* 7.2. http://psychology.wichita.edu/surl/usabilitynews/72/columns.htm (accessed December 12, 2007).

Bernard, Michael, Chia Hui Liao, and Melissa Mills. 2001. Effects of font type and size on the legibility and reading time of online text by older adults. Paper presented at ACM SIGCHI 2001. http://psychology.wichita.edu/surl/usabilitynews/3W/fontSR.htm (accessed December 12, 2007).

Blakeslee, Ann M., and Rachel Spilka. 2004. The state of research in technical communication. *Technical Communication Quarterly* 13 (1): 73-92.

Boekelder, Angelique, and Michael Steehouder. 1998. Selecting and switching: Some advantages of diagrams over tables and lists for presenting instructions. *IEEE Transactions on Professional Communication* 41 (4): 229-241.

Boekelder, Angelique, and Michael Steehouder. 1999. Switching from instructions to equipment: The effect of graphic design. In *Visual information for everyday use: Design and research perspectives*, ed.

Harm J. G. Zwaga, Theo Boersema, and Henriette C. M. Hoonout, 67-73. London: Taylor and Francis.

Botka, Dana Howard. 2002. From gobbledygook to plain English: How a large state agency took on the bureaucratic form letter. In *Proceedings: STC's 49th Annual Conference.* Society for Technical Communication. http://www.stc.org/ConfProceed/2002/PDFs/STC49-00022.pdf (accessed October 15, 2007).

Brumberger, Eva R. 2003a. The rhetoric of typography: The awareness and impact of typeface appropriateness. *Technical Communication* 50 (2): 224-231.

Brumberger, Eva R. 2003b. The rhetoric of typography: The persona of typeface and text. *Technical Communication* 50 (2): 206-223.

Brumberger, Eva R. 2004. The rhetoric of typography: Effects on reading time, reading comprehension, and perceptions of ethos. *Technical Communication* 51 (1): 13-24.

Burton, Susan. 2007. You may already be a technical communicator! *Intercom*, June, 4.

Carliner, Saul. 2006. Current challenges of research in information and document design. In *Information and document design: Variety on the research*, ed. Saul Carliner, Jan Piet Verckens, and Cathy de Waele, 1-24. Amsterdam, The Netherlands: John Benjamins.

Carroll, John M. 1990. *The Nurnberg Funnel: Designing minimalist instruction for practical computer skill.* Cambridge, MA: MIT Press.

Carroll, John M., ed. 1998. *Minimalism beyond the Nurnberg Funnel.* Cambridge, MA: The MIT Press.

Dixon, Peter. 1987. The processing of organizational and component step information in written directions. *Journal of Memory and Language* 6: 24-35.

Doumont, Jean-luc. 2002. Magical numbers: The seven-plus-or-minus-two myth. *IEEE Transactions on Professional Communication* 45 (2), 123-127.

Farkas, David K. 1999. The logical and rhetorical construction of procedural discourse. *Technical Communication* 46 (1): 42-54.

Felker, Daniel B., Marshall Atlas, Veda R. Charrow, V. Melissa Holland, Cheryl Olkes, Janice C. (Ginny) Redish, and Andrew M. Rose. 1980.

Document design: A review of the relevant research. Washington, DC: American Institutes for Research.

Felker, Daniel B., Frances Pickering, Veda R. Charrow, V. Melissa Holland, and Janice C. (Ginny) Redish. 1981. *Guidelines for document designers*. Washington, DC: American Institutes for Research.

Ganier, Frank. 2004. Factors affecting the processing of procedural instructions: Implications for document design. *IEEE Transactions on Professional Communication* 47 (1): 15-26.

Garvery, Philip M., Martin T. Pietrucha, and Donald Meeker. 1997. Effects of font and capitalization on legibility of guide signs. *Transportation Research Record* 1605: 73-79. http://clearviewhwy.com/ResearchAndDesign/researchWhitepapers.php (accessed December 6, 2007).

Gellevij, Mark, and Hans van der Meij. 2004. Empirical proof for presenting screen captures in software documentation. *Technical Communication* 51 (2): 224-238.

GMAP (Government Management Accountability & Performance). *General guidelines*. Plain Talk, http://www.accountability.wa.gov/plaintalk/ptguidelines/default.asp (accessed December 15, 2007).

Gregory, Judy. 2004. Writing for the web versus writing for print: Are they really so different? *Technical Communication* 51 (2): 276-285.

Hayhoe, George F. 2000. What do technical communicators need to know? *Technical Communication* 47 (2): 151-153.

Helvetica. 2007. Gary Hustwit. London: Swiss Dots.

HHS (Health and Human Services Department). 2006. *Research-Based Web Design & Usability Guidelines*. Usability.gov, http://usability.gov/pdfs/guidelines.html (accessed September 25, 2007).

Hofmann, Patrick. 2004. The successes and challenges of visual language. *Intercom*, June, 16-18.

Horton, William. 1991. *Illustrating computer documentation: The art of presenting information graphically on paper and online*. New York: Wiley.

Isakson, Carol S., and Jan H. Spyridakis. 1999. The influence of semantics and syntax on what readers remember. *Technical Communication* 46 (3): 366-381.

Larson, Kevin. 2004. The science of word recognition or how I learned to stop worrying and love the bouma. Advanced Reading Technology, Microsoft Corporation, http://www.microsoft.com/typography/ctfonts/WordRecognition.aspx (accessed December 6, 2007).

Locke, Joanne. 2004. A history of plain language in the United States government. PlainLanguage.gov, http://www.plainlanguage.gov/whatisPL/history/locke.cfm (accessed November 30, 2007).

Loorbach, Nicole, Joyce Karreman, and Michael Steehouder. 2007. Adding motivational elements to an instruction manual for seniors: Effects on usability and motivation. *Technical Communication* 54 (3): 343-358.

Mazur, Beth. 2000. Revisiting plain language. *Technical Communication* 47 (2): 205-211.

Meeker & Associates. Legibility. ClearviewHwy, http://clearviewhwy.com/ResearchAndDesign/legibilityStudies.php (accessed December 6, 2007).

Miller, George. 1956. The magical number seven, plus or minus two: Some limits on our capacity for processing information. http://www.musanim.com/miller1956 (accessed November 11, 2007). Originally published in *The Psychological Review*, 63 (1956): 81-97.

Mirel, Barbara, and Rachel Spilka. 2002. *Reshaping technical communication: New directions and challenges for the 21st century.* Mahwah, NJ: Lawrence Erlbaum Associates, Inc.

Morkes, John, and Jacob Nielsen. 1997. Concise, SCANNABLE, and objective: How to write for the Web. useit.com: Jakob Nielsen's Website, http://www.useit.com/papers/webwriting/writing.html (accessed November 30, 2007).

Morkes, John, and Jacob Nielsen. 1998. Applying writing guidelines to Web pages. useit.com: Jakob Nielsen's Website, http://www.useit.com/papers/webwriting/rewriting.html (accessed December 4, 2007).

Office of the Federal Register. 1998. Making regulations readable in *Document drafting handbook*, MMR-1-MMR-6. http://www.archives.gov/federal-register/write/plain-language/readable-regulations.pdf (accessed October 17, 2007).

PlainLanguage.gov. Federal plain language guidelines.
http://www.plainlanguage.gov/howto/guidelines/reader-friendly.cfm
(accessed October 15, 2007).

Poole, Alex. 2005. Which are more legible: Serif or sans serif typefaces?
Alex Poole Interaction design and research,
http://www.alexpoole.info/academic/literaturereview.html (accessed
October 4, 2007).

Redish, Janice C. (Ginny). 1988. Reading to learn to do. *Technical Writing Teacher* 15 (3): 223-233. Reprinted in *IEEE Transactions on Professional Communication* 32 (1989) (4): 289-293.

Redish, Janice C. (Ginny). 1993. Understanding readers. In *Techniques for Technical Communicators*, ed. Carol Barnum and Saul Carliner, 14–41. New York: Macmillan.

Redish, Janice C. (Ginny). 1998. Minimalism in technical communication. In *Minimalism Beyond the Nurnberg Funnel*, ed. John M. Carroll, 219-245. Cambridge: The MIT Press.

Redish, Janice C. (Ginny). 2000. What is information design? *Technical Communication* 47 (2): 163-166.

Redish, Janice C. (Ginny). 2004a. Applying research to practice: What's relevant today? Presentation at the annual conference of the Society for Technical Communication, May 9-12, in Baltimore, MD.
http://www.redish.net/content/handouts.html (accessed September 24, 2007).

Redish, Janice C. (Ginny). 2004b. Letting go of the words. *Intercom,* June, 5-10.

Redish, Janice C. (Ginny). 2006. Guidelines for writing clear instructions and messages for voters and poll workers. NIST (National Institute of Standards and Technology),
http://vote.nist.gov/032906PlainLanguageRpt.pdf (accessed September 17, 2007).

Redish, Janice C. (Ginny). 2007. *Letting go of the words*. San Francisco: Morgan Kaufmann.

Redish, Janice C. (Ginny). Headings. PlainLanguage.gov,
http://www.plainlanguage.gov/howto/guidelines/headings.cfm (accessed October 15, 2007).

Roebben, Nicolas, and Yves Bestgen. 2006. Reading and expertise: The impact of connectives on text comprehension in the financial field. In *Information and document design: Variety on the research*. Ed. Saul Carliner, Jan Piet Verckens, and Cathy de Waele, 149-165. Amsterdam, The Netherlands: John Benjamins.

Salvo, Michael, Meredith W. Zoetewey, and Kate Agena. 2007. A case of exhaustive documentation: Re-centering system-oriented organizations around user need. *Technical Communication* 54 (1): 46-57.

Schriver, Karen. A. 1997. *Dynamics in document design.* New York: John Wiley & Sons.

Securities and Exchange Commission. 1998. *A plain English handbook: How to create clear SEC disclosure document.* http://www.sec.gov/pdf/handbook.pdf (accessed December 10, 2007).

Spyridakis, Jan H. 2000. Guidelines for authoring comprehensible web pages and evaluating their success. *Technical Communication* 47 (3): 359-382.

Spyridakis, Jan H., Laura D. Schultz, and Alexandra L. Bartell. 2005. Heading frequency and comprehension: Studies of print versus online media. In *Proceedings: STC's 52nd Annual Conference*. Society for Technical Communication. http://www.stc.org/ConfProceed/2005/PDFs/0032.pdf (accessed November 28, 2007).

Spyridakis, Jan H., and Michael J. Wenger. 1992. Writing for human performance: Relating reading research to document design. *Technical Communication* 39 (2): 202-215.

Steehouder, Michael. 2004. Acquiring procedural knowledge of a technology interface: introduction to this special issue. *IEEE Transactions on Professional Communication* 47 (1): 1 – 4.

Steehouder, Michael F., and Carel J. M. Jansen. 1996. The sequential order of instructions: Impact on text quality. In *Proceedings: STC's 43rd Annual Conference*. Society for Technical Communication. http://www.stc.org/confproceed/1996/PDFs/PG247250.PDF (accessed October 04, 2007).

Taylor, Conrad. 2000. Information design: A European perspective. *Technical Communication* 47 (2): 167-168.

van der Meij, Hans, and Mark Gellevij. 1998. Screen captures in software documentation. *Technical Communication* 45 (4): 529-543.

van der Waarde, Karel. 1999. Typographic dimensions and conventional wisdom: A discrepancy? *Technical Communication* 46 (1): 67-74.

Wright, Patricia. 1988. Issues of content and presentation in document design. In *Handbook of human-computer interaction*, ed. M. Helander, 629-652. New York: North-Holland.

Wright, Patricia. 1998. Printed instructions: Can research make a difference? In *Visual information for everyday use: Design and research perspectives*, ed. Harm J. G. Zwaga, Theo Boersema, and Henriette C. M. Hoonout, 45-66. London: Taylor and Francis.

Zimmerman, Donald E. and Terri Prickett. 2000. A usability case study: Prospective students' use of a university web page. In *Proceedings: STC's 47th Annual Conference*. Society for Technical Communication. http://www.stc.org/ConfProceed/2000/PDFs/00099.pdf (accessed December 4, 2007).

Applying best practice in technical communication and information design
to documentation for poll workers

Prepared by

UsabilityWorks
453A Chestnut Street
San Francisco, California 94133

Dana E. Chisnell
Susan C. Becker

March , 2008

Contents

Applying best practice in technical communication and information design
to documentation for poll workers

Deliverable: A discussion of best practice in technical communication and information design and its implications for the VVSG (Voluntary Voting System Guidelines).

What is the focus of this report?

In this report, we discuss how best practices in technical communication and information design can be applied to the recommendations in the VVSG for poll workers and election judges.

VVSG provides general direction for usable documentation

The VVSG provides some direction for developing usable documentation for poll workers:

- Part 2: Documentation Requirements, section 4.4.6, states that documentation for pollworkers is covered in Part 1: Equipment Requirements (3.2.8).

- Part 1: Equipment Requirements, section 3.2.8: Usability for poll workers, primarily discusses the usability of the system. However, the requirements under 3.2.8.1-C: Documentation usability (through C.3) do provide some direction specifically for the quality, scope, target audience, usability, and content of the documentation.

- Part 1: Equipment Requirements, section 3.2.8-A: Clarity in system messages for poll workers, also points to Part 1:3.2.4 Cognitive issues. This section includes several guidelines for system instructions (though not specifically for documentation). The requirements under 3.2.4-C Plain Language (through C.7) cover using plain language as well as making warnings clear, putting the context before the action, using simple vocabulary, starting each instruction on a new line, writing instructions in the positive (telling the poll worker the correct way to do something rather than what not to do), using the imperative, and avoiding gender-based pronouns.

VVSG documentation requirements that are supplied are limited

The requirements provided by the VVSG support current best practices in technical communication and information design. However, they are lacking in several ways:

- The requirements specifically for documentation cover several best practices, but at a high level. They are limited and general.

- For the requirements to be testable, they need to be more specific. For example, it may be possible to review a document to determine if it includes "instructions…for setup, polling, and shutdown," but it would be difficult to test whether they are "clear, complete, and detailed."

- The requirements for system instructions are too general regarding the documentation for poll workers for several reasons, including that the audience of the system instructions is primarily voters rather than poll workers, system instructions are usually on a screen rather than printed, and system instructions cover voting rather than the poll workers' main tasks.

- The requirements for system instructions are directed to user interface designers rather than the people writing the user documentation.

- The requirements are located in the section on system instructions rather than in the section on documentation. The requirements that apply to voting system documentation for users bear repeating.

What VVSG requirements did we review?

We reviewed the Voluntary Voting System Guidelines Recommendations to the Election Assistance Commission (August 31, 2007), available from http://vote.nist.gov/vvsg-report.htm. We started with Part 2: Documentation Requirements and reviewed these sections:

- Part 2: Documentation Requirements. 4.4.6 Documentation for poll workers

- Part 1: Equipment Requirements. 3.2.8.1-C Documentation usability

  - 3.2.8.1-C.1 Poll Workers as target audience

  - 3.2.8.1-C.2 Usability at the polling place

  - 3.2.8.1-C.3 Enabling verification of correct operation

- Part 1: Equipment Requirements. 3.2.4-C Plain Language

  - 3.2.4-C.1 Clarity of warnings

  - 3.2.4-C.2 Context before action

  - 3.2.4-C.3 Simple vocabulary

  - 3.2.4-C.4 Start each instruction on a new line

  - 3.2.4-C.5 Use of positive

  - 3.2.4-C.6 Use of imperative voice

  - 3.2.4-C.7 Gender-based pronouns

What best practices did we rely on?

To ensure that we were not depending exclusively on writer's lore in evaluating voting system documentation for pollworkers, we first reviewed much of the extensive literature about technical communication and information design. Our report, *Review of relevant literature: technical communication and information design,* is available from NIST.

We also reviewed several sets of existing guidelines to understand the current thinking of professional communicators on what makes best practice. Many of those guidelines are evidence-based, as well. Our report, *Current guidelines: technical communication and information design*, is also available from NIST.

We developed a set of heuristics (with operationalizing questions) from a combination of the literature review and the review of existing guidelines. We based our review of the VVSG on these. They are listed in the appendix of this document.

What we found

VVSG recommendations for documentation for poll workers support best practice

We found that the four VVSG requirements that discuss documentation for poll workers are in agreement with best practice for technical communication and information design.

3.2.8.1-C Documentation usability

The system *SHALL* include clear, complete, and detailed instructions and messages for setup, polling, and shutdown.

Best practice:

- Understand your audience. Focus on the user's task rather than a comprehensive presentation of the system.

- Organize your document—logically, clearly, in order of use. Organize documents logically around the user's tasks rather than around the system.

- Use familiar, common words. Describe what the pollworker is doing rather than what the machine is doing.

- Use "you." Write procedural steps in the imperative.

- Put instructions in the order in which they must be completed.

- Start each instruction on a new line.

3.2.8.1-C.1 Poll Workers as target audience

The documentation required for normal system operation *SHALL* be presented at a level appropriate for non-expert poll workers.

Best practice:

- Understand your audience. Make the content relevant and appropriate for the audience.

- Use familiar, common words that pollworkers use.

- Use simple words. Use plain rather than formal words.

3.2.8.1-C.2 Usability at the polling place

The documentation *SHALL* be in a format suitable for practical use in the polling place.

Best practice:

- Understand your audience. Make the document appropriate for the circumstances.

- Use emphasis to highlight important information (but don't overdo it).

- Use mixed case (not all caps) in text and instructions.

- Use familiar fonts. Use a legible font size. Use appropriate line length and leading.

3.2.8.1-C.3 Enabling verification of correct operation

The instructions and messages *SHALL* enable the poll worker to verify that the system

> a. Has been set up correctly (setup);
> b. Is in correct working order to record votes (polling); and
> c. Has been shut down correctly (shutdown).

Best practice:

- Understand your audience. Focus on the user's task rather than a comprehensive presentation of the system.

- Organize your document—logically, clearly, in order of use. Organize documents logically around the user's tasks rather than around the system.

If instructions focus on the user's task, the "poll worker should not have to guess whether an operation has been performed correctly," as the VVSG suggests.

VVSG requirements for plain language also agree with best practice

We found that the VVSG requirements for system instructions that are discussed under cognitive issues (3.2.4) as plain language (3.2.4-C) are also in agreement with best practices for technical communication and information design.

3.2.4-C Plain Language

Instructional material for the voter *SHALL* conform to norms and best practices for plain language.

Best practice:

This requirement covers many of the best practices that we used for our review. We list here only the high level best practices rather than the specific heuristics.

- Organize the document to meet the audience's needs.

- Use simple, common words.

- Write clear sentences and paragraphs.

- Use lists.

- Use emphasis to highlight important information.

3.2.4-C.1 Clarity of warnings

Warnings and alerts issued by the voting system *SHOULD* clearly state:

       a. The nature of the problem;
       b. Whether the voter has performed or attempted an invalid operation or whether the voting equipment itself has   malfunctioned in some way; and
       c. The set of responses available to the voter.

Best practice:

- Understand your audience. Focus on the user's task rather than a comprehensive presentation of the system.

- Put warnings before—not after—consequences. Make warnings stand out without being separated from the text.

3.2.4-C.2 Context before action

When an instruction is based on a condition, the condition *SHOULD* be stated first, and then the action to be performed.

Best practice:

- Put instructions in the order in which they must be completed. Put phrases in an instruction in the order in which they must be processed.

- Put warnings before—not after—consequences.

3.2.4-C.3 Simple vocabulary

The system *SHOULD* use familiar, common words and avoid technical or specialized words that voters are not likely to understand.

Best practice:

- Use simple words. Use plain rather than formal words.

- Use familiar, common words (avoid jargon). Describe what the pollworker is doing rather than what the machine is doing. Use legal, foreign, and technical terms sparingly or only when necessary.

3.2.4-C.4 Start each instruction on a new line

The system *SHOULD* start the visual presentation of each new instruction on a new line.

Best practice: Start each instruction on a new line.

3.2.4-C.5 Use of positive

The system *SHOULD* issue instructions on the correct way to perform actions, rather than telling voters what not to do.

Best practice: Write short sentences. Write sentences in the positive.

3.2.4-C.6 Use of imperative voice

The system's instructions *SHOULD* address the voter directly rather than use passive voice constructions.

Best practice:

- Use "you." Write procedural steps in the imperative. Talk directly to readers rather than about them.

- Use active voice—most of the time.

3.2.4-C.7 Gender-based pronouns

The system *SHOULD* avoid the use of gender-based pronouns.

Best practice: We believed, erroneously, that the use of gender-based pronouns would no longer be a problem, and so did not include this guideline. This is an error that we plan to rectify.

VVSG requirements can support usable documentation by covering best practices more thoroughly

VVSG requirements cover only some documentation best practices

The four VVSG requirements for document usability for pollworkers all come under the best practice of understanding your audience. Most technical writers and information designers agree that understanding your audience and focusing on their tasks is the most important guideline and the foundation of all good user documentation. The VVSG also covers several other important best practices, for example, using simple, common words, but it could be more comprehensive.

VVSG requirements cover best practices at a high level

The requirement to use plain language covers many guidelines. Here, too, most technical writers and information designers, especially those involved in making government documents readable and usable, would agree with the importance of plain language. But the VVSG does not include the details that writers need to follow this practice.

VVSG system requirements apply to system instructions, not poll worker documentation

The VVSG requirements for system instructions discussed under cognitive issues related to plain language are in agreement with many of the best practices in technical communication and information design. However, because the requirements apply to the system, the end user of the instructions is the voter, not the poll workers.

Systems requirements are written for a technical audience. Technical communicators are a separate audience, which could benefit from further guidance from the VVSG. The VVSG can be helpful for people who are striving to write usable documentation.

Existing documentation requirements are difficult to test

The more general the guideline, the more difficult it is to test. Because the four VVSG requirements for document usability for pollworkers do not include the more specific guidelines, the usability of the documents may be difficult to test.

The requirements to minimize cognitive issues are more specific and so more testable, but they are directed at the system rather than the poll worker documentation.

Conclusion

The VVSG requirements provide a basic framework for writing and developing usable documentation for poll workers. To be effective, the VVSG must be expanded to:

- Include a broader range of documentation best practices as requirements

- Define more specific and usable directions to technical communicators and information developers

- Describe documentation best practices that can be realistically implemented and evaluated

Understand your audience

- Does the document focus on the user's task rather than a comprehensive presentation of the system?

- Does the document address separate audiences separately?

- Is the content relevant and appropriate for the audience?

- Is the document appropriate for the circumstances?

Organize the document to meet the audience's needs

Organize your document—logically, clearly, in order of use

- Is the document organized logically around the user's tasks rather than around the system?

- Is the document organized by a time sequence when appropriate?

- Is the document organized by relevance when appropriate? Are first things put first?

- Does the document include clear "navigation": headers, footers, page numbers, index, table of contents, tabs?

Use headings

- Does the document use the appropriate number of headings to break up the text?

- Are the headings descriptive and informative?

- Do the headings focus on the user rather than the system?

- Do the headings stand out?

Use topic sentences

- Does the first sentence of a paragraph tell the readers what they're going to read about?

- Are procedures introduced with a topic sentence or phrase when appropriate? (For example, To set up the ballot box:…)

- Is the context set (briefly) before the action? (This should not be confused with an inappropriately long overview.)

Use simple, common words

Use simple words

- Does the document use simple words and avoid difficult words?

- Does the document use plain rather than formal words?

- Does the document avoid unnecessary words?

- Are the words used concrete rather than abstract as much as possible?

Use familiar, common words (avoid jargon)

- Does the document use familiar, common words that pollworkers use?

- Do the words describe what the pollworker is doing rather than what the machine is doing (as appropriate)?

- Are legal, foreign, and technical terms used sparingly or only when necessary? Are they explained?

- Are abbreviations and acronyms used sparingly and defined when used?

Use "you"

- Are procedural steps written in the imperative?

- Do descriptions of the user's actions use "you"?

- Are the assumed readers the pollworkers? Does the document talk directly to them rather than about them?

Write clear sentences and paragraphs

Write short sentences

- Is each instruction as short as possible?

- Are sentences as short as possible?

- Are the connections between sentences clear?

- Are the subject and verb close together in sentences?

- Does the main idea come first in sentences, before exceptions and conditions?

- Is important information in the main clause (an independent clause) in sentences?

- Are embedded clauses at the end of sentences rather than in the middle?

- Are sentences written in the positive (rather than with multiple negatives)?

Write short paragraphs

- Do paragraphs make one point—have one main idea only?

Use active voice—most of the time

- Are instructions written in the active voice?

- Is passive voice used when appropriate (focus is on the object or it doesn't matter who is doing the action)?

Use lists

Use vertical lists

- Does the document use lists for related items whenever possible to break up blocks of text?

- Do lists of equal items use bullets and lists of sequential or ordered items use numbers?

- Are items in lists parallel in structure?

Place important information at the top of bulleted lists

- Are the most important items at the top of bullet lists?

- Are lists introduced with a phrase or sentence as appropriate to set the context?

Put instructions in the order in which they must be completed

- Are instructions in the order in which they must be completed? Is the first task first and the last, last?

- Are phrases in an instruction in the order in which they must be processed?

- Are procedures introduced with a phrase or sentence as appropriate to set the context?

Put warnings before—not after—consequences

- Do warnings come immediately before actions that will lead to the consequences the warning describes (not after or all together at the beginning of the document or section or procedure)?

- Do warnings stand out without being separated from the text?

Start each instruction on a new line

- Does each instruction start on a new line?

Use graphics

- Does the document use graphics like photographs and diagrams to show physical objects and relationships?

- Is the relationship between the graphics and the text clear?

- Are the graphics near the appropriate text?

- Do the titles of the graphics, if used, match the task and the text? Is the terminology consistent?

- Do the graphics illustrate the instructions rather than the objects?

- Do graphics show only what is necessary? (Are just the appropriate parts of the object illustrated?)

- Are items on graphics identified with callouts or labels?

- Are arrows or other markings used to indicate the direction of movement in graphics?

- Are graphical perspectives (the reader's orientation to the graphic) helpful? ("a viewpoint above, in front of, and slightly to one side of the object")

- Are tables used for quantitative data? Do tables have clear headings and labels?

- Are screenshots used in software discussions to help identify objects and verify states?

- As with other graphics, are screenshots labeled and are only relevant parts shown or emphasized?

- Is the visual narrative, when used, complete (steps are not left out)?

Design documents for easy reading

Use mixed case (not all caps) in text and instructions

- Is mixed case rather than all caps used in text and instructions?
- Is bold rather than all caps used to show emphasis?

Use emphasis to highlight important information (but don't overdo it)

- Is important information highlighted or emphasized with bold or italics?
- Is emphasizing used sparingly?

Use familiar fonts

- Are the fonts familiar?
- Are the fonts legible (approximately 12 pt)?
- Are the font styles limited to two or three?
- Are the lines a reasonable length (8 or 9 words a line)?
- Is the leading appropriate (1 to 4 points)?

Use ragged-right margins

- Are the margins ragged-right?
- If justified text is used, are the words spaced without "rivers'?

Test your documents

www.ingramcontent.com/pod-product-compliance
Lightning Source LLC
Chambersburg PA
CBHW080410290526
45791CB00008BA/2223